iMac

2023

USER GUIDE

**The Complete Step By Step Manual
With Practical Instructions To Teach
Beginners & Seniors How To Master
The New iMac With M3 Chip. With
Pictures, Tricks And Hacks**

By

Howard Yeager

DISCLAIMER:

The information contained in this book is for educational purposes only. All efforts have been executed to present accurate, reliable, and up-to-date information. No warranties of any kind are implied. The contents of this book are derived from various sources. Please consult a licensed professional before attempting any techniques contained herein.

By reading this document, the reader agrees that under no circumstances is the author responsible for any losses, direct or indirect, which are incurred as a result of the information contained in this book including errors, omissions, and inaccuracy.

Table of Contents

Introduction 1

    Release Date 2

    Price 3

    Design 3

    Display 4

    M3 CPU And Other Specifications 6

    Camera 8

    Ports 8

Chapter One 10

    The Mac's Menu Bar 10

        Picking From Apple's Menu 10

        Settings Screens 11

        Your Mac Status 11

        Spotlight 12

        The Control Center 12

        Siri 12

        Center For Alerts 12

    Use Spotlight To Search 12

        Try To Search 13

        Use Spotlight For Arithmetic 15

Mac's Preferences Pane 17

   Invoke The Command Menu 18

   Modify Main Menu Settings 19

Activate Siri For Mac 20

   Activate Siri.. 21

   Disable Siri... 24

Open Notification Center 24

   Use Mac's Notification Center Widgets 27

Make Use Of Mac's Dock.............................. 28

   Use The Dock To Access Files........................ 28

   Modify The Dock's Contents......................... 29

   Make Changes To The Dock 31

Chapter Two.. 33

Launch Internet Explorer On Your Mac 33

   Connect Via Wi-Fi...................................... 33

   Employ Ethernet... 33

   The Use Of Instant Hotspot.......................... 34

   Modify Your Files Using Quick Look Feature. 34

Record Your Mac Screen 38

   Capture Screenshots Or Screen Recordings ... 38

   Use The Shortcut Keys To Snap Some Photos 41

Raise Or Lower The Brightness 43

   Make Use Of The Light-Control Buttons 43

   Manually Adjusting The Brightness 44

Adjust the volume on your Mac 44

   Make Use Of Mac's Trackpad 45

   Mouse Pointer Actions....................................45

   Clicks And Points 46

Macs With Touch ID 46

   Authorize Touch ID 47

   Pay Using Touch ID On Your iPhone 50

Produce Paperwork Using Your Mac 51

   Adapt The Way You Print Documents............54

Make Use Of The Shortcut Keys........................55

   The Keyboard Shortcuts For Mac 56

   Change The Shortcut Keys..............................57

   Turn Off A Shortcut Key 58

Run Software On A Mac 59

   Mac Window Management Tools 60

   Using The Program's Full-Screen Mode.........65

   Split View Your Mac's Applications 67

Chapter Three 71

The Desktop Manager For Mac 71

    Adjust Stage Manager's On/Off Switch 72

    Adapt Stage Manager's Preferences 74

Find Programs And Safari Add-Ons 75

    Look For And Purchase App 76

Set Up Mac App Store Purchases 80

    Reinstall Your Software 81

    Application Installation, And Removal 81

Make Use Of A Mac For Your Document 83

    Make Some Paperwork 84

    Layout Paperwork 85

    Read Files On A Mac 87

    Make Notes In Mac Documents 89

    Create A Single PDF From Many Mac Files 94

Use Stacks To Organize Your Files 96

    Start Your Computer Stacks 97

    Modify The Way Desktop Icons Look 99

Create Folders To Store Documents 99

    Set Up A File System 100

    Transfer File To The Folder 101

    Combining Two Similar-Named Folders 102

Chapter Four 104

Tag Your Files For Easy Organization 104

Classify Data In Storage 105

Locate Tagged Items 106

Use The Mac's Time Machine 108

Retrieve Mac Time Machine Backups 111

Change Your Mac's Settings 113

Alter The Desktop Background On Your Mac 115

Mac Widget Creation And Modification 117

Embellish Your Desktop With Widgets 119

Boost Notification Center With Widgets 119

Make Your Widgets 120

Set Preferences For The Widget 122

Put Your Mac Into Screen Saver Mode 123

Adjust Your Mac's Screen Saver 123

Include A Mac User / Group 125

Make A Group 128

Access Your Online Accounts 129

App-Based Account Creation 130

Modify Your Account's Settings And
Information 132

Delete Your Online Profile 133

Explore The Mac's Gallery For Shortcuts......... 134

View The Exhibition By Opening It 134

Create A Quick Link To Your Gallery........... 135

Explore The Exhibits 135

Chapter Five.. 137

Make A Memoji With Messages App............... 137

Modify Your Mac's Profile Image 138

Modify Your Mac's Language Settings..........141

Increase The Size Of Text 144

Activate Focus On Mac.................................... 148

Replace Or Omit A Focus............................. 149

Pick Which Alerts To Receive 150

Create A Personal Screen Time Schedule 158

Enter Text By Voice On Your Mac.................... 160

Launch Dictation 161

Provide A Script.. 162

Configure The Keyboard Shortcut For Dictation
.... 164

Swap Out The Dictation Microphone 165

Disable Dictation 166

Use Mac Mail To Send An Email..................... 166

Email It Over 166

Keep An Unfinished Draft 167

Set Up A Future Email.............................. 168

Using A Mac Rely Messages 169

Chapter Six... 173

Make And Receive Video Calls 173

Use Facetime For A Video Chat 174

Join A Facetime Video Chat......................... 174

Turn Down A Facetime Video Chat 175

Photo Editing On The Mac 176

Alter A Video Or Picture 176

Make A Photocopy 178

Revisions By Cut-And-Paste 179

Delete Your Changes................................... 180

Extract And Reuse Text From Images..............181

Create A Note In A Hurry On A Mac 183

Use Maps To Get Instructions......................... 185

Get Direction 186

Get Direction Automatically 190

How Does Family Sharing Work? 191

Initiate Mac Family Sharing 192

How To Limit A Child's Computer Use 197

Use Family Sharing To Share Purchases......... 200

    Disabling Purchase Sharing........................ 204

Coordinate Your Work Across Devices 205

    Airdrop... 206

    Mac Airplay.. 206

    Markup For Continuity...............................207

    Sketch Of Continuity.................................207

    Handoff...207

    Rapid Connectivity 207

    Communicating Via Telephone 207

    Sidecar 208

    Universal Clipboard................................... 208

    Universal Control....................................... 208

Put The iPhone Camera As A Webcam 209

    First things first 209

    Convert Your iPhone Into A Webcam........... 210

    Invoke The iPhone's Camera Instantly......... 212

    Start The Video And Activate Desk View...... 213

Wirelessly Transmit Media From Your Mac 214

    Put On Your Preferred Headphones............. 215

Control Your Mac And iPad 217

Pair Your Mac With A Nearby Device........... 218

Separate Your Mac From All Other Gadgets 220

Disable The Global Lockdown System..........220

Using Apple's Handoff................................. 221

Use Watch Approval System For Your Mac..223

Use Facetime On Your Mac.............................226

Make Calls From Your Mac's Applications...227

Use Your Mac To Take Calls 229

Control Facetime Call On Your Mac.............230

Control Your Apple ID Preferences 231

Put Your Mac's Files In iCloud Drive 234

Create A Drive In iCloud...............................234

Collaborate On Data With Others.................237

Delete A Shared Folder Or File.....................244

Introduction

Apple's latest M3 CPU gives the 24-inch iMac a performance boost.

With the M3 processor and up to 2x quicker speed, this stunningly slim all-in-one with a huge 4.5K Retina display becomes the greatest in the world.At its Spring Loaded event in April 2021, Apple debuted a revamped iMac with a bright new look and an M1 processor. It wasn't until October 2023 that the M3 processor was introduced as the first major upgrade. Detailed information regarding the 2023 iMac is provided below.

Release Date

On October 30 (almost 30 months after the release of the M1), Apple held a "Scary Fast" Mac event and unveiled the M3 iMac. The new M3 iMac may be ordered today for November 7th delivery.

If Apple keeps to the same schedule, we may not see an updated 24-inch iMac until 2026.

Price

As with the M1 model, the M3 iMacs start at $1,299/£1,399 (the U.K. price remains the same as it was with the January 2023 hike of £150 compared to the M1 launch price-we had thought Apple would alter pricing when iPhone prices were lowered outside the U.S. but alas it hasn't). additional advanced models with additional storage and networking connections are available for a price of $1,699/£1,799 and £1,499/$1,599, respectively.

Design

With the release of the updated iMac in 2021, Apple stepped up the all-in-one design by offering a wider variety of dual-color choices and a bigger 24-inch screen that was still remarkably thin at 11.5mm (0.45 inches).

A height-adjustable stand and a less prominent chin are among the changes we want to see in the future, although they are still a ways off. The brand-new M3 iMac looks and feels just like the M1 model. While the anticipated 27-inch iMac has yet to be officially announced, Apple has introduced a new Space Black color for the MacBook Pro.

Display

The 4.5K Retina display, anti-reflective coating, 500 nits of brightness, and True Tone are all features of the 24-inch iMac. As a more premium feature, ProMotion would be welcome on the iMac, but it will probably not be implemented until the bigger iMac or iMac Pro.

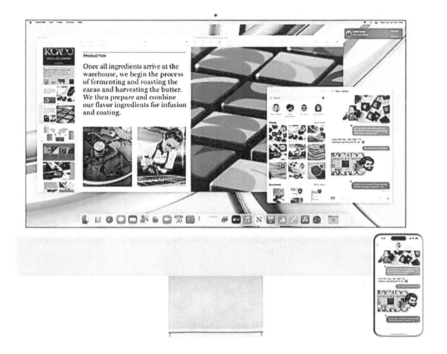

Now that the M3 model has been released, it will likely be at least two years until a new model emerges. Apple may eventually increase the screen size to 25 inches by shrinking the bezels and adding a notch for the FaceTime camera, as it does with the MacBooks.

M3 CPU And Other Specifications

The M1 iMac included an 8-core processor, a GPU with up to 8 cores, and 16GB of RAM. The M3 is Apple's successor to the M2, and it has the following improvements over its predecessor:

- Dual-core and quad-core processors, totaling 8 cores.
- GPU with 8 processing cores
- Ray tracing with hardware acceleration
- Neural Processor, 16-Core
- Bandwidth of 100 GB/s for Memory
- Amounts of Memory: 8GB, 16GB, and 24GB

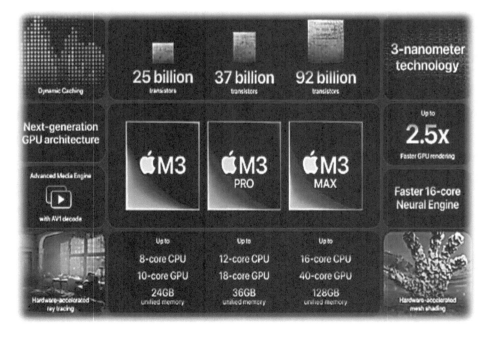

It looks quite similar to Apple's M2, but the company says the M2 is far quicker and has superior graphics. A faster Neural Engine, ProRes encoding and decoding, and AV1 capabilities are also included.

	M2	M3
Standard	8 CPU cores (4 high-performance and 4 energy-efficient) 8 or 10 GPU cores	8 CPU cores (4 high-performance and 4 energy-efficient) 8 or 10 GPU cores
Pro	10 or 12 CPU cores (6 or 8 high-performance and 4 energy-efficient) 16 or 19 GPU cores	11 or 12 CPU cores (5 or 6 high-performance and 6 energy-efficient) 14 or 18 GPU cores
Max	12 CPU cores (8 high-performance and 4 energy-efficient) 30 or 38 core GPU cores	14 or 16 CPU cores (10 or 12 high-performance and 4 energy-efficient) 30 or 40 GPU cores

The jump from M1 to M3 is rather larger:

7 CPU cores, 8 GPU cores, 256 GB of storage, and 8 GB of unified memory. We have now reached the era of the 8-core CPU, 8-core GPU, 256GB SSD, and 8GB DDR4 RAM.

- Used to have a 256GB hard drive, 8GB of RAM, and a CPU with 8 cores. Now with 8 CPU cores, 10 GPU cores, 256 GB of storage, and 8 GB of unified memory.
- Was: 8-core CPU, 8-core GPU, 512GB storage, 8GB unified memory. Now with 8-core CPU and 10-core GPU, 512GB of storage, and 8GB of unified memory.
- Apple updated the other M2 Macs earlier this year with the same Wi-Fi 6E and Bluetooth 5.3 features.

Camera

The M3 iMac contains the same 1080p FaceTime HD camera in the M1 variant. The iMac lacks the modern capabilities we were expecting for, such as Center Stage and wide-angle.

Ports

There are two Thunderbolt/USB 4 ports and a 3.5mm headphone jack on the base model M3 iMac, with four on the higher-end variants. The power adapter for the more expensive versions has a built-in Gigabit ethernet connector, which is standard on the more expensive configurations but costs an additional $30 on the base model. The iMac's small design precludes the addition of modern features like HDMI or an SDXC card port seen on the MacBook Pro and Mac Studio.

Chapter One

The Mac's Menu Bar

Exactly what does a Mac's menu bar consist of?

The menu bar runs along the top of the screen on your Mac. To choose actions, complete tasks, and see progress, use the menus and icons on the top bar.

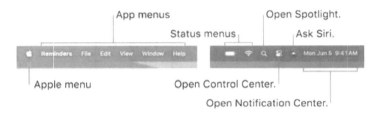

A bar includes options. The Apple menu and app menus may be seen on the left. Spotlight, Control Center, Siri, and the Notification Center may all be found on the right side of the screen.

The menu bar may be hidden by default and shown only when the mouse is moved to the top of the screen.

Picking From Apple's Menu

Common actions like updating software, accessing System Preferences, locking the screen, and powering down your Mac can all be accessed from the Apple menu in the upper left corner of the screen.

Settings Screens

Alongside the Apple menu are App Store menus. The application's name will be bold, followed by general options like "File," "Edit," "Format," and "Window." App-specific instructions are easy to find in the "Help" section.

Each menu has choices; most applications support some. The File menu in many applications includes Open.

Your Mac Status

The far-right status menu icons allow you to monitor your Mac's battery life and adjust keyboard brightness.

Status menu icons provide further information or alternatives. Select Wi-Fi to see networks, then Display to activate Dark Mode and Night Shift. Fully customizable menu.

Drag an icon while holding Command to rearrange the status menu. Holding down the Command key and dragging the status menu icon off the menu bar removes it easily.

Spotlight

Click Spotlight in the menu bar to search Mac and web. Search using Spotlight.

The Control Center

When you launch Control Center by tapping its icon, you'll have quick access to frequently-used functions like AirDrop, AirPlay, Focus, and many more. For more information on how to manage your account, see here.

Siri

Selecting the Siri emblem in the menu bar lets you ask Siri to access files or apps or search locally or online.

Center For Alerts

Click the date and time in the top right corner of the menu bar to open the Notification Center, where you can check missed notifications, appointments, notes, and the weather. Check the Notification Hub.

Use Spotlight To Search

Spotlight is a useful tool for rapidly locating objects on your Mac, such as programs, files, and emails. News, sports scores, the current weather, stock prices, and more may all be accessed via Siri Suggestions. Spotlight can even make computations and conversions for you.

Say to Siri, "How many centimeters are there in an inch?" as in "What does parboil mean?"

Try To Search

1. Perform one of the following actions on your Mac:

   - If the Spotlight symbol is there in the navigation bar, click it.
   - Press the Command-Space bar.
   - Use the keyboard's function keys (if they exist).

   Moving the Spotlight window about the desktop is simple.

   If the Spotlight icon isn't already there, you can add it using Control Center.

   Simply enter your query into the search bar and watch as relevant results pop up instantly.

2. When using Spotlight, the most relevant results are shown first. Spotlight will show you suggested alternatives to your search both locally and online.

View search results in Spotlight.

View search results on the web.

Click a top hit to preview or open the item.

View search results in an app.

Spotlight window with the search bar at the top and the results at the bottom.

3. You may do one of the following with the output:
   - Check out the Spotlight search results for this suggestion: Select the highlighted item by clicking on it.
   - Check out the results of this recommended online search: To go forward, choose the desired item and then click the arrow button.
   - Release the seal: You should double-click it. You may also choose it and hit the Return key.

- An application like Messages or the Help Viewer could launch when you do this.
- To activate or deactivate a feature, just use Spotlight to find it, then click the toggle switch next to its name.
- Quickly do an activity, such as making a FaceTime call or sending an email, by typing a phone number, email address, date, or time.
- Display the file's directory on your Mac: To open a file by holding down the Command key while selecting it. The file's path is shown in the preview's footer.
- Just a copy: Move a file by dragging it to the desktop or a Finder window.
- Check out all the outcomes in the Finder on your Mac: Click Search in Finder at the very bottom of the results list.

The Screen Time feature dims app icons in search results and displays a clock when you're not actively using them or when you've reached the time limit you set for each app.

Use Spotlight For Arithmetic

Use Spotlight for all your arithmetic and converting needs.

In the Spotlight search bar, you may input a mathematical expression, currency amount, temperature, and more to obtain a conversion or computation instantly.

The Spotlight window with a desired conversion weight is entered in the search bar and the resulting weights are shown below.

- Calculations: Enter a numeric expression, such as (956*23.94) or (2020/15), to search for.
- Changes in currency: If you want to convert 300 krone to euros, for example, enter "300 krone in euros."
- Input a temperature to convert it, such as "340K in F" or "98.8F." or "32C." or "98.8F."

- Convert measurements: Enter 25 lbs, 54 yards, 23 stone, or "32 ft to meters."
- Type in a place and the words "world clock" will convert the time to the local time in that area, such as "time in Paris" or "Japan local time."

Spotlight searches may be refined to include or exclude certain folders, disks, or categories of data (such as emails or messages).

You may disable Siri Suggestions for Spotlight if you want Spotlight to search just the information on your Mac and not the web.

Mac's Preferences Pane

Key features of macOS, such as AirDrop, Wi-Fi, and Focus, may be quickly accessed via the Mac's Control Center. Accessibility shortcuts, battery life, and quick user switching are just a few examples of what you may add to Control Center.

If you click the Control Center icon in the menu bar and see an orange dot, it means your Mac's microphone is active; a green dot means your camera is; and an arrow means your location is being used. A green dot indicates the simultaneous usage of a microphone and camera. You may be able to see which applications are accessing your microphone, location, and camera in the field at the top of the Control Center. If you want to learn more about your privacy settings (macOS 13.3 or later), you may do so by clicking that box.

Click an icon to turn an item on or off.

Click to open or close Control Center.

Microphone and location indicators

Click to see more information.

For some controls, click to see more options.
For Stage Manger, click to turn it on or off.

The screen's top-right corner houses the device's Control Center, where you can access features including Wi-Fi, Focus, Sound, and the Now Playing screen.

Invoke The Command Menu

1. Select System Preferences from your Mac's menu.

2. Use the elements in the Control Center to do any of the following:
   - A Mac's volume, for instance, may be changed by dragging the Sound slider up or down.
   - To activate or deactivate a function, such as AirDrop or Bluetooth®, click the corresponding icon.
   - To access the corresponding submenu, click the item's name or arrow. For instance, clicking "Focus" will bring up your Focus list, where you may toggle Focuses on and off.

TIP: Drag frequently used items from the Control Center to the menu bar for easy access. Drag the item off the menu bar while holding down Command to remove it.

Modify Main Menu Settings

1. Select System Preferences from the Apple menu, and then select the Control Center button in the sidebar. (You may have to scroll down a little.)
2. Modify the options in the corresponding tabs on the right.
   - Control Center Modules: Items in this section are always displayed and cannot be deleted. You may also display them in the menu bar. Choose from the pop-up menu when you click an item.

- You may add more modules to your Control Panel and main menu. Change the switches beneath each item as required. Certain configurations may have more choices.
- From the menu bar, you can adjust the clock and add Spotlight, Siri, Time Machine, and VPN connection status.

Activate Siri For Mac

You can use Siri on your Mac to perform common things like schedule an appointment, launch an app, or look up information quickly.

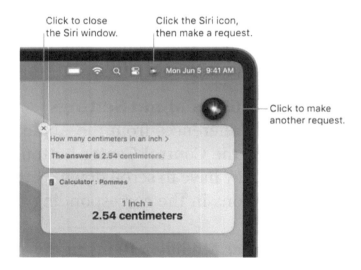

A screenshot of a Macintosh computer's top right corner displaying the Siri icon in the menu bar and the resulting Siri window with the question "How

many centimeters are there in an inch?" and the answer (the conversion from Calculator). To make a second request, open Siri by clicking the button in the window's upper right corner. Click the close button to dismiss the Siri window.

Activate Siri

1. Select Siri & Spotlight in the left pane of System Preferences by going to Apple > System Preferences on your Mac. (You may have to scroll down a little.)
2. Activate Ask Siri by toggling its switch to the right if it isn't already.
   If Siri is not enabled and you attempt to use it, you will be asked to do so. If you want to utilize Siri, you'll need to be online.
3. You may do one of the following when prompted to enhance Siri or Dictation:
   - Disseminate recorded audio: If you want Apple to keep recordings of your Mac's Siri and Dictation conversations, you may do so by selecting Share Audio Recordings. A piece of saved audio might be reviewed by Apple.
   - Don't talk about the podcast you heard: Please do not proceed at this time.

     Select Apple menu > System Settings > Privacy & Security if you decide you wish to start or stop sharing audio recordings. (You may have to scroll down a little.) To enable or disable the Enhance Siri & Dictation feature, go to Analytics & Enhancements on the right.

You may remove the audio conversations at any time since they are tied to a unique random identifier and are older than six months.

4. Take any of these actions:
   - Use "Hey Siri" or "Siri" to activate Siri on your device and language if "Listen for" is enabled. This option, together with "Allow Siri when locked," lets you use Siri on a locked or sleeping Mac.
   - Choose an existing or create a keyboard shortcut to activate Siri by opening the "Keyboard shortcut" menu and selecting its button.
   - If your device has a row of function keys, press and hold the Microphone key to activate Siri or the keyboard shortcut.
   - Siri's voice may be changed in several ways. Choose a language from the dropdown. Select "Siri voice" and then your preferred voice from the Voice Variety and Siri Voice menus

to hear a sample. Some languages have just one option.

- To quiet Siri, click Siri Responses and disable "Voice feedback". She'll answer in Siri, but you won't hear her.
- Display Siri's responses: Go to Siri Responses > display Captions > Always to activate "Always show Siri captions."
- Display your speech on the screen. Select Siri's responses and select "Always show speech."

Select Apple > System Settings > Control Center in the left pane to bring Siri to the main menu. (You may have to scroll down a little.) Select Menu Bar Only on the right, then tap the ellipses next to Siri and select Show in Menu Bar.

Siri On/Off
Siri requires an active internet connection.

1. Any of the following will enable Siri on your Mac:
   - If you have a function key row, you may utilize the shortcut for Siri and Spotlight by pressing and holding the Microphone key.
   - Select Siri from the main menu. You may add it using the Control Center's preferences if it's not already there.

- If your Mac has a Touch Bar, you can access Siri by pressing the button there.
- Just use the "Hey Siri" or "Siri" command (if it has been enabled in Siri & Spotlight settings).

2. Make a request—for example, "Set up a meeting at 9" or "What was the score for last night's game?"

If you have Location Services enabled, the location of your device at the moment you submit a request will be calculated.

Disable Siri

1. Select Siri & Spotlight in the left pane of System Preferences by going to Apple > System Preferences on your Mac. (You may have to scroll down a little.)
2. On the right, you may disable Ask Siri.

If you're the family organizer for a Family Sharing group, you may set up Screen Time for a kid and limit access to Siri & Dictation.

Open Notification Center

Mac's Notification Center lets you examine missed alerts and display widgets for things like calendar events, birthdays, the weather, and news without leaving your desktop.

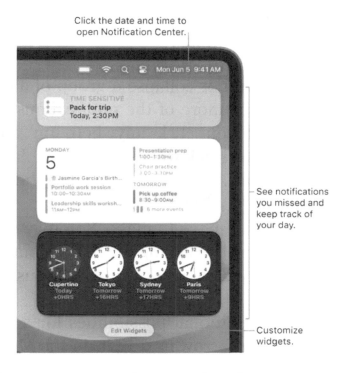

Click the date and time to open Notification Center.

TIME SENSITIVE
Pack for trip
Today, 2:30 PM

See notifications you missed and keep track of your day.

Customize widgets.

Notification Center alerts and widgets.

Mac's Notification Center may be opened and closed.

Perform any of the following on your Mac:

- Launch the Alerts Menu: To change the time and date, either use the trackpad's buttons to the left of the screen or click the menu bar's date and time.
- Anywhere on the desktop, the date and time in the menu bar, or a two-finger swipe to the right on a trackpad will close Notification Center.

To respond to a notice in the notice Center, hover the cursor over it.

- You may expand or collapse a group of alerts by selecting one or more of the notifications within the group. If you click anywhere on the top notification, the stack will expand to display all of the notifications. To hide the pile, use the option to "Show less."
- Act on it: Pick a move to make. You may dismiss a Calendar alert by clicking the Snooze button, or you can respond to an email alert by using the Reply button.
  If you want additional possibilities for a certain action, click the arrow next to it. In the Messages app, for instance, you may respond to a call by tapping the down arrow next to Decline and selecting Reply with Message.
- For more reading: To access the content in question, just tap the notice. If a down arrow appears to the right of the app's name, tapping it will expand the notice to provide more information.
- If an arrow appears to the right of an app's name, tapping it brings up a menu from which you may mute notifications, disable them altogether, or access the app's Notifications settings.

- You may erase a single alert or the whole stack. It's time to hit Clear/Clear All.

Use Mac's Notification Center Widgets

You may perform any of the following in the Notification Center:

- For more reading: To access the widget's associated settings, app, or web page, just click anywhere within it. By way of illustration, you may access the Date & Time settings by clicking on the Clock widget, the Reminders app by clicking on the Reminders widget, and the Weather widget by clicking on the browser and accessing the full forecast there.
- Widget resizing: Select a widget, right-click with Control, and select a new size.
- To delete a widget, select it with the mouse, hold the Option key down, and then click the Remove button.

Notification Center widgets may be arranged in a variety of ways.

Tip: If you need to reduce distractions by silencing all alerts—or allowing just some messages to appear—use a Focus, such as Do Not Disturb or Work.

Make Use Of Mac's Dock

The Dock is a handy spot on the Mac desktop to access frequently used applications and services like Launchpad and Trash.

App icons, a Downloads stack, and the Trash can appear on the Dock.

There's a downloads folder and room for three recently used applications if they aren't already in the Dock. By default, the Dock is positioned along the bottom border of the screen, but you may specify an option to display it along the left or right side instead.

Use The Dock To Access Files

You may accomplish any of the following on your Mac's Dock:

- To launch an application, just tap its icon. To launch the Finder, for instance, choose it from the Dock and click on it.
- When you launch an application and choose a file, you can: Simply drop the document onto the app's icon. To see a document made in Pages, for

instance, just drag it onto the Pages icon on the Dock.

- Display a Finder item: Use the button to right-click the icon.
- To close the current app and return to the previous one: Select the app's icon with the option click.
- Close all other applications and switch to the one you want to use: To switch applications, press and hold the Option key while clicking the command button.

Alter what you're doing using Dock items

You may accomplish any of the following on your Mac's Dock:

- Show a drop-down list of commands: You can open a file by clicking on its name or performing an action like "Show Recent" that appears when you control-click an item.
- If an application stops responding, you may force it to close by right-clicking its icon and selecting Force Quit (unsaved work may be lost).

Modify The Dock's Contents

Perform any of the following on your Mac:

- Put something in the Dock. You may organize your most recently used applications by dragging them to the left side of the line. You may organize your recently used applications by dragging and dropping files and folders to the right side of the other line. The item's alias is added to the Dock.

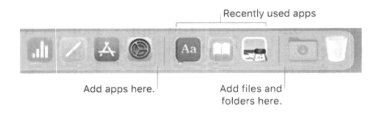

Separator lines before and after the recently used applications area may be seen at the right end of the Dock.

You may see your folders stacked on the Dock after you move them there. The Downloads folder is pre-created on the Dock.

- Drag an item from the Dock until Remove appears. The original file or folder is still there; just the alias has been deleted.

The software itself is still on your Mac, so even if you delete the icon from the Dock by mistake, you can easily add it back. Launch the program to restore its Dock icon. Select Options > Keep in Dock by Control-clicking the app's icon.

- Move an item to a new Dock slot by dragging it there.

The icon for the app now being used on your iPhone, iPad, iPod touch, or Apple Watch will show up in the rightmost corner of the Dock.

Make Changes To The Dock

1. Select System Preferences from the Apple menu, and then select Desktop & Dock in the left pane. (You may have to scroll down a little.)
2. Modify the settings to your liking below Dock on the right.

   For example, you may modify how objects display in the Dock, vary their size, place them along the left or right border of the screen, or even conceal them.

   The window's Help tab may be accessed by clicking the question mark icon.

Quickly change the Dock's size by dragging the cursor over the Dock's divider line until two arrows appear, then clicking and dragging in either direction. By right-clicking (Control-clicking on Mac) the delimiter, further options will appear.

The Dock may be accessed by shortcut keys. Press Fn-Control-F3 to go to the Dock. Then, use the Left and Right Arrow keys to navigate between the various icons. To activate an item, press Return.

If an app or System Preferences icon in the Dock has a red badge, you have unfinished business with that tool. If you have fresh mail, for instance, the Mail app logo in the Dock will become red.

Chapter Two

Launch Internet Explorer On Your Mac

If you have a Mac, you can use it to access the web wherever you go. Wi-Fi (wireless) and Ethernet (wired) connections are two of the most prevalent methods to access the internet. If you can't find either, an Instant Hotspot may be your next best option.

Connect Via Wi-Fi

The Wi-Fi symbol appears in the top menu when connected to a wireless network. Select a network to join by clicking the icon. If a padlock appears next to a network's name, entering the password is required to connect to that Wi-Fi network.

Employ Ethernet

Ethernet may be accessed via a direct Ethernet connection, or a digital subscriber line (DSL) or cable modem. If your Mac has an Ethernet port (represented by a jack), you may use it to connect to the network. Connecting an Ethernet cable to a Mac without a dedicated Ethernet port is possible with the help of an adapter that lets you utilize a USB or Thunderbolt connection instead.

The Use Of Instant Hotspot

You may use your iPhone or iPad as a personal hotspot with your Mac with Instant Hotspot if you don't have access to Wi-Fi or Ethernet.

Everywhere you go, everywhere you are

When relaxing at home: A Wi-Fi or Ethernet internet connection might be provided by your ISP. If you are unsure about your access type, contact your Internet service provider (ISP).

Your workplace provides you with access to a Wi-Fi or Ethernet network. For information on how to access and make use of the corporate network, please contact your firm's IT department or network administrator.

Wi-Fi hotspots (public wireless networks) and Apple's Instant Hotspot feature (assuming both your Mac and your phone carrier allow it) are useful while you're on the road. It's important to remember that using certain public Wi-Fi networks may include entering a password, agreeing to terms of service, or making a financial contribution.

Modify Your Files Using Quick Look Feature

Open and modify your files using Mac's Quick Look feature

Quick Look allows you to **quickly** examine a full-size preview of practically any **file** type without actually opening it. Quick Look allows you to edit photographs, videos, and **audio** files without leaving the window.

Quick Look window displays a picture with options to annotate, rotate, and share, as well as open the image in the Preview program.

Quick Look may be used to search for text in Finder windows, on the desktop, in messages, and other locations.

1. To select many objects at once on a Mac, hit the Space bar.

   There's a new Quick Look window up. The most recently picked item will be shown first if several items were chosen.

2. Try out any of these options in the Quick Look pane:
   - Resize the window: Drag the corners of the window. The Quick Look window also has a Full-Screen button, accessible from the menu in the upper left. To return to regular viewing mode, just drag the mouse cursor to the window's bottom right corner and click the Exit Full-Screen button that appears.
   - You may adjust the size of a picture by using the plus (+) or minus (-) keys on your keyboard.
   - To rotate an object, either hit the Option key and then click the Rotate Left button, or click the Rotate Right button while holding down the Option key. To keep turning the object, keep clicking on it.
   - Add a price tag: Select Markup and press Enter. Make notes in the files.
   - To trim an audio or video file, select it and then use the yellow handles to move it along

the trimming bar. Select Play to preview the modifications. The Revert button may be used to return to a previous state. When you're ready to save your work, choose Done and decide whether to overwrite or make a new copy of the file.

- Look through the things (if you've chosen more than one): To go left or right, use the left and right arrow buttons or the keyboard shortcuts. To see the slideshow in full screen, use the Play button.
- Display things in a grid (if numerous were selected): Press Command Return to open the index sheet.
- Release the seal: Select Open in [Application] to proceed.
- To share an item, click the Share button and then choose the appropriate sharing method.
- If the object is a screenshot or a photo, you may cut off the backdrop and copy only the topic. A copy subject menu option will appear when you right-click the picture. Copy the topic and paste it into your next document, email, text, or note.
3. When you're finished using Quick Look, you may dismiss it by using the Space bar or clicking the Close button.

The video component of a Live Photo instantly begins playing when you access it in the Quick Look window. To see it again, click Live Photo in the bottom-left corner of the photo.

Record Your Mac Screen
Record your Mac screen or take screenshots

Screenshot and other keyboard keys allow you to capture images (screenshots) and video of your Mac's display. The screenshot is a panel of tools that allows you to quickly and simply capture screenshots and screen recordings with granular control over what is captured (e.g., by delaying the capture for a certain amount of time or including the mouse pointer or mouse clicks).

Capture Screenshots Or Screen Recordings
Screenshot allows you to capture screenshots or screen recordings.

1. To access Screenshot on a Mac, use Shift-Command-5 (or look it up in Launchpad).

This is the Screenshot menu.

2. To choose what you want to capture or record, click the appropriate tool (or use the Touch Bar).

The frame may be dragged to a new location on the screen, or its borders can be dragged to make the selected region larger or smaller.

Action	Tool
Capture the entire screen	
Capture a window	
Capture a portion of the screen	
Record the entire screen	
Record a portion of the screen	

3. If you wish to change the settings, choose the Options tab.

Whether you're taking a screenshot or recording your screen, the available choices will be different. A delay may be specified, the mouse cursor or clicks can be shown, and the file can be saved to a location of your choosing.

The Show Floating Thumbnail feature allows you to more efficiently work with a finished shot or recording by temporarily displaying a thumbnail of the media in the bottom-right corner of the screen for a few seconds before saving it to the destination you chose.

4. Initiate the screen capture or recording:
   - Choose a region or the whole screen and hit the Capture button.
   - To choose a window, point to it and press the mouse button.
   - To begin a recording, choose the Record option. Select the Stop Recording option from the main menu to end the recording.

While the thumbnail is temporarily shown in the lower-right corner of the screen when Show Floating Thumbnail is on, you may perform any of the following:

   - Simply swipe right to permanently delete the file.
   - Just drop the thumbnail anywhere you need it, whether it is a Word doc, an email, a note, or a Finder window.

- A new window will pop up when you click the thumbnail, allowing you to annotate the screenshot, cut the video, and share it.

A program might launch if that's where you saved the screenshot or recording.

Use The Shortcut Keys To Snap Some Photos
Taking screenshots on a Mac may be done using a variety of shortcut keys. The documents are dropped onto the hard drive.

Use the Control key in conjunction with the other keys to copy a screenshot and paste it somewhere, such as an email or another device. To replicate the whole screen, for instance, you would use the shortcut Shift-Command-Control-3.

Action	Shortcut
Capture the entire screen	Press Shift-Command-3.
Capture a portion of the screen	Press Shift-Command-4, and then move the crosshair pointer to where you want to start the screenshot. Pre. the mouse or trackpad button, drag over the area you want to capture, then release the mouse or trackpad button.
Capture a window or the menu bar	Press Shift-Command-4, and then press the Space bar Move the camera pointer over the window or the men bar to highlight it, and then click.
Capture a menu and menu items	Open the menu, press Shift-Command-4, and then dr. the pointer over the menu items you want to capture.
Open Screenshot	Press Shift-Command 5.
Capture the Touch Bar	Press Shift-Command-6.

These shortcuts may be altered by the user under the Keyboard options. Select Screenshots from the Apple menu > System Settings > Keyboard > Keyboard Shortcuts on the right. (You may have to scroll down a little.)

Screenshots are stored as .png files and screen recordings are saved as .mov files. A screenshot or screen recording will have a filename that begins with "Screenshot" or "Screen recording" followed by the time and date.

Some programs, like DVD Player, may not allow you to capture images of windows.

Raise Or Lower The Brightness

Raise or lower the brightness of your Mac's screen

Both manual and automatic brightness adjustments are available for the screen.

Make Use Of The Light-Control Buttons

The brightness of your screen may be changed if you find it too bright or dim.

- To adjust the brightness of your Mac, use the corresponding keys or the Control Bar.

Brightness will be adjusted automatically.

1. To access the ambient light sensor on a Mac, choose Apple > System Settings > Displays. (You may have to scroll down a little.)
2. Activate the setting to "Automatically adjust brightness" on the right.

Manually adjusting the brightness is an option if you don't see an "Automatically adjust brightness" option.

Manually Adjusting The Brightness

1. To access the Mac's display settings, choose Apple menu > System Settings > Displays. (You may have to scroll down a little.)
2. Adjust the screen's brightness by dragging the Brightness slider to the right.

You may also have access to a Contrast slider to modify the display's contrast, depending on the monitor you've connected to your Mac.

Refer to your display's manual for more details on how to adjust the brightness settings.

Adjust the volume on your Mac

You may adjust the volume on your Mac by:

- You may either use the Control Strip or the volume keys on your keyboard. For instant volume control, press, for instance.
- Drag the volume slider after clicking the Sound option in the menu bar or Control Center.

  If the Sound control isn't on the menu bar, pick Apple menu > System Settings, then click Control

Center in the sidebar. (You may have to scroll down a little.) To toggle whether Sound appears in the menu bar at all times or just when it is active, click the arrow next to it on the right and choose the appropriate option.

- Adjust the volume using the Apple TV app's in-app controls.

Make Use Of Mac's Trackpad

Take use of Mac's trackpad and mouse movements

Click, touch, pinch, and swipe are just some of the motions you may use with a Mac with an Apple trackpad or Magic Mouse to do tasks like zooming in on documents, navigating music or web sites, rotating photographs, and accessing the Notification Center.

Mouse Pointer Actions

You may do a variety of actions with your fingers on your trackpad, including clicking, tapping, sliding, and swiping. To flip between pages, for instance, use a left or right swipe of two fingers.

- Select Apple menu > System Settings > Trackpad to see the available trackpad gestures and a short movie illustrating each one. (You may have to scroll down a little.)

In the Trackpad settings, you may also disable or alter the available motions.

Clicks And Points

To manipulate the mouse's interface, touch, slide, or swipe with one or more fingers. For instance, you can flip across pages by swiping your finger left or right.

- Select Apple menu > System Settings > Mouse in the sidebar to see the available mouse movements and a short movie illustrating each one. (You may have to scroll down a little.)

  Mouse preferences also allow you to disable or alter gesture functionality.

Macs With Touch ID

Touch ID allows you to securely unlock your Mac, make purchases from the iTunes Store, App Store, and Apple Books, and shop online with Apple Pay if your Mac or Magic Keyboard supports it. Some third-party applications also support Touch ID login.

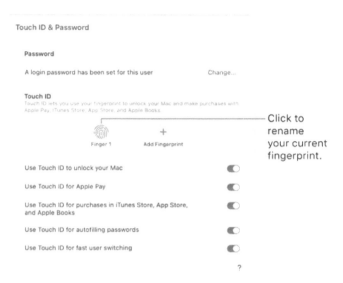

Touch ID & Password

Password

A login password has been set for this user   Change...

Touch ID
Touch ID lets you use your fingerprint to unlock your Mac and make purchases with
Apple Pay, iTunes Store, App Store, and Apple Books.

Finger 1   Add Fingerprint   Click to rename your current fingerprint.

Use Touch ID to unlock your Mac

Use Touch ID for Apple Pay

Use Touch ID for purchases in iTunes Store, App Store, and Apple Books

Use Touch ID for autofilling passwords

Use Touch ID for fast user switching

?

Configure Touch ID and Password Lock on your Mac, so that your fingerprint may be used to unlock it.

Authorize Touch ID

1. To enable Touch ID and a password on your Mac, choose Apple menu > System Settings. (You may have to scroll down a little.)
2. To add a fingerprint, choose Add Fingerprint, input your password, and then proceed with the on-screen prompts.

   Touch ID sensors, found on Macs and the Magic Keyboard, are placed in the upper right corner of the keyboard. Your Mac can save up to five fingerprints, but only three may be associated with your user account.

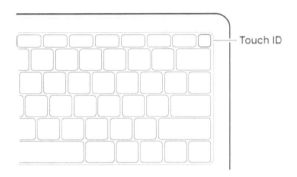

The Touch ID fingerprint sensor on a Touch ID keyboard is located in the upper right.

3. Pick your preferred method of using Touch ID:
   - Wake this Mac from sleep and use Touch ID to unlock it.
   - If you're using Apple Pay on this Mac, you may authenticate using Touch ID to finish your transactions.
   - iTunes, Apple Books, and the App Store: You may use Touch ID to buy anything from the Apple online shops right from this Mac.
   - Password autofill: Touch ID may be used to instantly enter a username, password, or credit card number when prompted in Safari or other applications.

- Switching between users on this Mac is quick and easy using Touch ID.

Fingerprints may be renamed or deleted.
1. To enable Touch ID and a password on your Mac, choose Apple menu > System Settings. (You may have to scroll down a little.)
2. Take any of these actions:
   - To give a fingerprint a new name, choose the text just underneath it and type the new name in.
   - Fingerprint removal: The steps are as follows: choose a fingerprint, input your password, unlock it, and delete it.

You can log on, unlock your Mac, and swap users all using your fingerprint.

You need to be logged onto your Mac with your password before you can utilize Touch ID for these actions.

- Your Mac and some password-protected objects may be unlocked by placing a finger on Touch ID when prompted to do so.
- Sign in using the login screen: Select your user name in the login box and then use Touch ID to log in.

Touch ID can only be used to access accounts that have a password. Guest users and those who are limited to sharing cannot utilize Touch ID.

- To switch users, press Touch ID after clicking the quick user switching option in the top bar.

You need to have quick user switching enabled, and the user you want to switch to must have already signed in to the Mac with a password before you can use Touch ID to switch to them.

Pay Using Touch ID On Your iPhone

1. Enter your password to log in to your Mac.
2. Make a purchase from the Apple Online Store or with Apple Pay.
3. When prompted, place your finger on Touch ID.

Report issues with Touch ID

- If you're having trouble using Touch ID, try making sure your finger is clean and dry before trying again. Fingerprint recognition may be impacted by factors such as moisture, lotions, wounds, and dry skin.
- To ensure security, you must enter your password before starting your Mac. Touch ID requires a password entry on certain devices. For instance, after five unsuccessful passwords or

fingerprint tries or every 48 hours, users are required to reenter their password.

Users can only see their Touch ID data once signed in, and administrators can't make any changes to a user's fingerprints or Touch ID settings.

Produce Paperwork Using Your Mac

To customize how a file is printed on paper, use your Mac's Print dialog to choose a printer and adjust print settings.

1. Select File > Print from the menu bar or use the shortcut Command-P to print a document.

   A preview of your manuscript in print form appears in the Print dialogue.

   The Print dialogue choices may vary based on the printer and the app you're using. If the instructions below don't match what you're seeing, choose Help from the menu bar to see the application's documentation.

Your print job settings and a preview will be shown in the Print dialogue.

A full-size preview may be seen by selecting Open PDF in Preview from the PDF preview menu.

2. If everything in the Print dialog box seems OK, you can just press Print to finish. If not, go on to the next step.

- Printer: Pick your preferred printing device. You can always install a printer if there isn't one already.
- Presets are collections of customized printing options. You may use the default settings for most print jobs, but you also have the option

to choose a stored set of parameters from a previous print job.

- Please enter the desired quantity of copies. If you want to print every page of a document before making another copy, go to "Paper Handling" and then "Collate Sheets."

- Select the Pages to Print: Indicate the pages you want to print. You may choose which pages to print or print the whole document. If you have a document that is 10 pages long, you may print pages 6-9. The Selection option allows you to print just a subset of the pages in the range. To print a specific page, click its label in the Preview panel. Pages in your selection don't have to be in a continuous range. Page 2 and page 4 of a 5-page document, for instance, may be printed separately.

- If your printer supports color printing, choose to print in color. When disabled, only black and white copies of the document will be produced.

- Select On from the Double-Sided pop-up option to print on both sides of the paper if your printer supports it. If you want your document to be bound at the top of each page when printing, choose On (Short Edge) in the print menu.

- Select a paper size to print your document. If you have 8.5 by 11-inch paper in the printer, choose US Letter.
- You may choose between portrait and landscape by using the buttons provided. You can see the effect of your edits on the preview pages to the right.
- To scale the printed picture to the paper size, enter a percentage here. You can see the update in the new sidebar previews.

3. Select Print from the File menu.

Adapt The Way You Print Documents

The following are some typical uses for a printer:

- Pick the paper size you'd want to use for the printout.
- You may save commonly used print preferences for easy future usage.
- Adjust the size of text and pictures so that they fit on a page.
- Use two sides of the paper.
- Use the specified paper tray for printing.
- One sheet may hold numerous pages or pictures.

- You may print the pages in whatever sequence you choose, including odd and even.
- Bordered, inverted, or otherwise unconventionally printed pages

Clipped text or unusually large margins when printing a document might be the result of a mismatch between the app's margin settings for your page size and the nonprintable region of the page specified for your chosen printer. Try adjusting the page size such that there is no blank space.

Make Use Of The Shortcut Keys

Keyboard shortcuts are combinations of keys that may be used to do a job fast on a Mac. Keyboard shortcuts involve one or more modifier keys (such as Caps Lock or Control) and a final key, hit at the same time. To open a new window without having to navigate the menus, you may just hit the Command and N keys.

Keyboard shortcuts may be modified or turned off entirely.

Your Mac's language and keyboard layout may affect the shortcuts you use in programs. Check the app menus in the menu bar for the proper shortcuts if the ones below don't perform what you want. You may also use the Keyboard Viewer to inspect your current keyboard layout, known as an input source.

The Keyboard Shortcuts For Mac

In macOS applications, keyboard shortcuts may be found right next to menu options. Many shortcuts for the keyboard are consistent across programs.

Keyboard shortcuts

Symbols represent modifier keys.

In Finder, clicking the Edit menu will provide keyboard shortcuts for its contents.

Many macOS applications' help files contain a rundown of their most useful keyboard shortcuts.

Execute actions with the use of keyboard shortcuts

- To use a keyboard shortcut, hit the final key of the sequence while holding down a modifier key (such as Caps Lock, Command, or Control).

  To paste copied text, press and hold the Command key and the V key, as in "Command-V," until both keys are released at the same time.

Change The Shortcut Keys

Some shortcuts on the keyboard are modifiable by altering the key combinations used.

1. To customize your Mac's keyboard shortcuts, choose Apple > System Settings > Keyboard (you may need to scroll down), and then select Keyboard Shortcuts on the right.
2. You may choose a section, such as "Mission Control" or "Spotlight," from the list on the left.

   Clicking the App Shortcuts category on the left will allow you to alter the keyboard shortcuts for individual programs.

3. Click the box next to the keyboard shortcut you wish to edit in the list on the right.
4. To change the active key combination, double-click it and then press the new combination.

Key combinations are limited to a single usage of each key type (for example, a letter key).

5. To make the new keyboard shortcut active, close all open programs and launch them again.

New keyboard shortcuts won't function if they duplicate keyboard shortcuts for other commands or apps. Whether it's your new shortcut or the previous one, you'll need to modify it.

Simply go to Keyboard Settings > Keyboard Shortcuts > Restore Defaults in the bottom-left corner to revert all shortcut keys to their original configuration.

Turn Off A Shortcut Key

Sometimes a keyboard shortcut in one program may clash with another shortcut in macOS. If this occurs, you may stop using that keyboard shortcut on macOS.

1. To customize your Mac's keyboard shortcuts, choose Apple > System Settings > Keyboard (you may need to scroll down), and then select Keyboard Shortcuts on the right.
2. You may choose a section, such as "Mission Control" or "Spotlight," from the list on the left.

3. Uncheck the box next to the shortcut in the list on the right to remove it.

Run Software On A Mac

You can leave many applications running in the background on a Mac. This is particularly helpful for regularly used programs like Safari and Mail.

The easiest method to launch an app on your Mac is to click the program's icon in the Dock.

Click an app icon to open the app.

In the Dock, you'll see Safari's icon.

There are alternative methods to launch the program on a Mac without clicking its icon in the Dock.

- To access your apps, open Launchpad from the Dock's menu.
- Ask Siri to launch a program for you. Put in a command like "Open Calculator." Refer to Siri.

- To launch an application, choose Spotlight from the menu bar, type the name of the program, then hit Return.
- Choose the Apple menu > Recent Items > the app you last used.
- To launch an application, double-click the Finder icon on the Dock, then go to the Applications folder using the Finder window's sidebar.

Mac Window Management Tools

On a Mac, a window appears whenever you launch an application or the Finder. Only one app may be running at a time, and when you hover over the menu bar, you'll see the app's name (bolded) and its menu options.

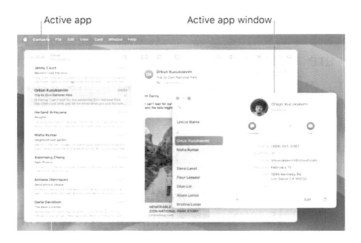

An illustration of a desktop with many windows open but no active ones.

Use numerous windows or several sorts of windows in programs like Safari and Mail. On macOS, you may shut a single window or all of them using a variety of methods.

Arrange, combine, and resize program windows

Perform any of the following on your Mac:

- To reposition a window by hand, click and drag its title bar to the new location. Not all windows can be shifted around.
- If you want to shift a window to the left or right side of the screen, you may do it by holding down the Option key while you click and drag the green button in the upper left corner of the window. The window occupies that half of the screen; the menu bar and Dock remain visible.

  To restore the window to its former location and size, press and hold the Option key, drag the cursor over the green button, and then pick Revert.

- You can get windows to line up with one other by dragging one of them close to another; the two will snap into place without overlapping as they go closer. Multiple windows may be placed side by side.

To make two windows the same size, drag the edge you wish to enlarge until it coincides with the edge of the neighboring window and stops.

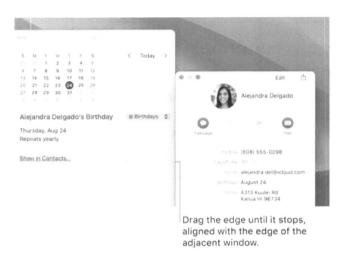

Drag the edge until it stops, aligned with the edge of the adjacent window.

Two windows lined up side by side by sliding one window's edge toward the other until it stops.

- Consolidate many windows into one tabbed interface: Click Window > Merge All Windows inside the program. Only the currently selected window type is merged when several window types exist inside a single program (like Mail's reader and new message windows).

Choose Window > Move Tab to New Window or just drag the tab out of the window to make it its window again.

Adjust the size of open windows

Use a window on your Mac to do any of the following:

- To make a window fill the whole screen, you may maximize it by holding the Option key and clicking the green button in the upper left corner of the app window. Click the button again while holding down the Option key to restore the window to its former size.

  If the Zoom option is selected in Desktop & Dock preferences, double-clicking an app's title bar will also cause the window to expand to its full width.

- To reduce the size of a window, use the Command+M keyboard shortcut or the yellow minimize button in the upper left corner.

  By default, windows don't minimize when you double-click their title bars, but you may change this behavior under Desktop & Dock.

You can alter the size of most windows by hand. You may make a window wider by dragging its edge (top, bottom, or side) or by double-clicking an edge.

Fast window hopping between apps

Perform any of the following on your Mac:

63

- Return to the previous application with Command-Tab.
- Click and hold the Command key, click Tab, then use the Left or Right arrow key to navigate among all running applications. Release the Command key.
- If you change your mind about switching applications while scrolling, press Esc or Period, then release Command.

Close a single window

Perform any of the following on your Mac:

- To close a single window, either click the red X in the upper left corner of the window or use the Command + W keyboard shortcut.
- Put an app to sleep by closing all its windows: To use, hit Option Command-W.

When you close all windows for an app, the app itself stays open (as seen by the little dot below the app's icon in the Dock), even if you close the app's windows. Pressing Command-Q will end the application. Apps to delete are listed here.

To temporarily hide the current program, hit the Command-H shortcut.

You can quickly find the open window or workspace you need by stacking them in a single layer using Mission Control.

Using The Program's Full-Screen Mode

You may make the most of your Mac's screen real estate and focus on your work without being distracted by the desktop by using the program's full-screen mode, which causes the app to take up the whole display.

1. To enter full-screen mode on a Mac, drag the cursor to the top left corner of the window and either click the green button or choose Enter Full Screen from the menu that displays.

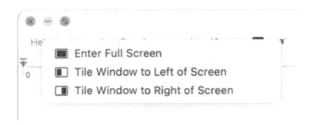

A window's context menu is shown when the mouse is hovered on the window's green title bar. Selecting "Enter Full Screen," "Tile Window to Left of Screen," and "Tile Window to Right of Screen" from the menu are examples of "top to bottom" navigation.

2. Try one of the following in full-screen mode:
   - Move the cursor to the top of the screen to reveal or conceal the menu bar. When the option to toggle the visibility of the menu bar in full-screen mode is disabled, the menu bar remains visible at all times.
   - The Dock may be shown or concealed by pointing at it or away from it.
   - Switch between applications without losing your place: Swipe left or right on the trackpad using three or four fingers, depending on how you configured your trackpad settings.
3. Back out of full-screen mode by clicking the green button again or by selecting Exit Full Screen from the menu that displays.

By maximizing a window, you may work in a larger window without switching to full-screen mode. The window will grow in size, but the toolbars and Dock will still be accessible. See also, how to resize app windows.

You may rapidly switch to Split View from full-screen mode to operate two apps at once. To use Split View, open Mission Control by pressing Control+Up Arrow (or swiping up with three or four fingers), then move a window from Mission Control onto the thumbnail of the full-screen app in the

Spaces bar. You may also combine program windows by dragging their thumbnails into the Spaces bar.

Split View Your Mac's Applications

Split View, which allows you to use two applications on your Mac side by side, is supported by many programs.

Split View, with Mail on the left and Photos on the right.

1. Mac users may tile windows to the left or right of the screen by clicking the green button in the top left corner and selecting the appropriate option from the menu.

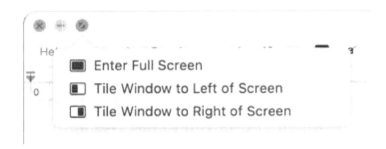

A window's context menu is shown when the mouse is hovered on the window's green title bar. Selecting "Enter Full Screen," "Tile Window to Left of Screen," and "Tile Window to Right of Screen" from the menu are examples of "top to bottom" navigation.

2. To switch to the second program, use the button on the other side of the display.
   The Split View opens in a separate window on the computer's screen.

3. You may accomplish any of the following in Split View:
   - To expose or hide the menu bar, move the pointer to the top of the screen. When the full-screen menu bar visibility option is deactivated, it is always visible.
   - The Dock may be shown or hidden by pointing at or away from it.

- Display or hide window title and toolbar: Click the window's title bar and drag the mouse to maximize or shrink it.
- To expand one side, move the mouse pointer to the left or right on the vertical bar in the middle. Double-clicking the dividing bar resets the sizes.
- Flip the window by dragging its title or toolbar to the opposite side.
- One side needs a different app: To switch windows, choose the one you want, then click the green button in the top left corner and select Replace Tiled Window. Click the desktop to return if you change your mind about changing the current window.
- Click the window's title bar and hover over the green button in the upper left corner to minimize it to the desktop. The software has a desktop shortcut.
- Press Control Up Arrow (or swipe up with 3-4 fingers) to access Mission Control. Select the app from the Spaces bar to return to Split View.
- Click a window, hover over the green icon in the top left corner, and choose Make Window Full Screen to maximize it.

- Press Control Up Arrow (or swipe up with 3-4 fingers) to access Mission Control. Select the app from the Spaces bar to return to Split View.

You may switch to Split View, where you can use two apps at once, from inside the app you now have full screen. To use Split View, open Mission Control by pressing Control+Up Arrow (or swiping up with three or four fingers), then move a window from Mission Control onto the thumbnail of the full-screen app in the Spaces bar. The Spaces bar also allows you to merge app thumbnails by dragging one onto another.

The "Displays have separate Spaces" option in Desktop & Dock has to be activated before Split View may be used across multiple screens.

Chapter Three

The Desktop Manager For Mac

Stage Manager is a desktop manager for Mac computers.

On your Mac, utilize Stage Manager to keep the program you're working with front and center, and your desktop clutter-free. The window you're now working in should take up most of the screen, while your recently used applications should line the left side.

Move, resize, and overlap windows to create a customized workspace. Stage Manager also allows you to join applications together on the screen for collaborative work. When you choose a folder, all of its associated applications will be brought to the front.

Stage Manager on a desktop with four programs in the recently used apps list on the left and a single app window in the middle.

Adjust Stage Manager's On/Off Switch

Switching between Stage Manager and regular windows is a breeze, so you can choose the workflow that works best for you.

Perform one of the following actions on your Mac:

- Select System Preferences from the Apple menu, and then select Desktop & Dock in the left pane. (You may have to scroll down a little.) To activate or deactivate Stage Manager, choose it from the right-hand Desktop & Stage Manager menu.
- To activate or deactivate Stage Manager, go to the Control Center via the menu bar.

72

Stage Manager should be used

Perform any of the following on your Mac:

- To switch applications, choose one from the list on the left.
- Adjust window placement, size, and overlap to improve efficiency.
- Apps may be grouped by dragging them from the left side of the screen to the group in the middle.
- To ungroup applications, just drag one of them to the left side of the screen.

Disabling Stage Manager's "Show recent apps in Stage Manager" option hides the left-hand list of installed programs. To display it, move the cursor to the screen's left edge.

Prove or conceal Use the menu option "Stage Manager"

There is always a Stage Manager on hand in the Control Room. It's optionally shown in the main menu.

1. Select System Preferences from the Apple menu, and then select the Control Center button in the sidebar. (You may have to scroll down a little.)
2. Select Stage Manager, and then either Show in Menu Bar or Hide in Menu Bar from the resulting drop-down menu.

Adapt Stage Manager's Preferences

1. Select System Preferences from the Apple menu, and then select Desktop & Dock in the left pane. (You may have to scroll down a little.)

2. In the right-hand menu, choose Desktop & Stage Manager.

3. The boxes adjacent to Show Items: may be checked or unchecked.

   - Exhibit content from the desktop.
   - Display the contents of the desktop in Stage Manager.

   When this switch is off, the contents of the desktop are concealed; you may reveal them by clicking the desktop.

4. Select an option from the pop-up menu that appears after clicking the "Click wallpaper to reveal desktop" button.

   - Always: clicking the wallpaper will minimize all open windows, revealing your desktop's icons and other desktop widgets.
   - You can only see your desktop objects and widgets by using Stage Manager and then clicking the background.

5. Activate or deactivate Stage Manager.

6. Toggle the "Show recent apps in Stage Manager" setting on or off.

If you disable this setting, your most frequently used applications will be hidden until you move the mouse cursor to the left side of the screen.

7. Select an item from the pop-up menu that appears after clicking "Show windows from an application"

- Without any delay: When selecting an app, all of its windows should be shown.
- When switching between applications, just the currently active window will be shown.

  When this is not selected, clicking the app on the left again will transition to the next accessible window.

Find Programs And Safari Add-Ons

The Mac App Store is where you can find programs and Safari add-ons.

Search the software Store or peruse its categories to locate the ideal software or Safari add-on. Once you've located what you're looking for, you may pay with your Apple ID or use a download code or gift card to get it.

Browse these areas for apps.

Browse for Safari extensions.

The Safari add-on is listed on the Mac App Store. Links to additional sections, such as "Discover," "Arcade," "Create," "Work," "Play," "Develop," "Categories," and "Updates," may be found in the sidebar on the left. Add-ons that can be used with Safari appear on the right.

Look For And Purchase App

1. You may accomplish any of the following on the Mac App Store:

   - Try to find a program: To search for an app, use the search bar at the upper left of the App Store screen and hit the Return key.
   - Check out the App Store by using the navigation bar on the left to choose Discover, Create, Work, Play, Develop, or Categories.

76

Mac systems with Apple hardware may run apps labeled as "Designed for iPhone" or "Designed for iPad."

2. If you click on the app's name or icon, you'll be able to read a summary of the app, check out user reviews, and learn how the app handles user data.

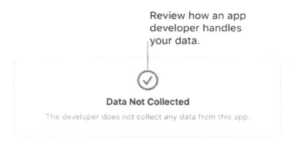

Review how an app developer handles your data.

Data Not Collected

The developer does not collect any data from this app.

A snippet of the main Mac program Store page displaying the developer's privacy policy for the chosen program.

3. Tap the "Get" or "Price" button to pay for and download the app. After that, you may utilize Touch ID or install the app by clicking the button again.

To halt a download during installation, click the progress indicator. Select Continue Download from the menu to continue.

A download may be halted at any time before it's complete:

- The Locator Says: To delete an application, right-click its icon in the Applications folder and choose Delete.
- From Launchpad: Press and hold the app icon, then click the Close button.

Modify your payment and download preferences.

1. Select System Preferences from the Apple menu, and then look for the section labeled "[your name]" toward the top of the sidebar.
   To input your Apple ID or create one, choose "Sign in with your Apple ID" if your name doesn't appear.
2. Select the "Media & Buys" tab.
3. Make a decision.

Use a download code, iTunes, or Apple Music gift card.

- To redeem a gift card in the Mac App Store, go to the top right corner, click your name, and then click Redeem Gift Card. Type in the download code or gift card number.

You may use your Mac's built-in camera to scan the barcode on a gift card if the card has a box around the code. Hold the gift card 4–7 inches (10–18 cm) from the camera after clicking Redeem and selecting Use Camera. Keep the card firm until the code is redeemed, and position the preview area such that the code is near the middle.

In-app items and memberships may be bought.

You may buy in-app purchases, additional game content, and subscriptions from certain applications. Enter your Apple ID credentials (or utilize Touch ID) to purchase the app.

Share and use your loved ones' app purchases

Members of a Family Sharing group may share their bought applications.

1. To access your account in the Mac App Store, click your name, or Sign In if you haven't already.
2. Select a relative from the "Purchased by" drop-down menu.
3. Click the Download icon next to an item.

Click Apple Menu > System Settings, then [your name] at the top of the sidebar, then Media & Purchases, and finally your desired settings.

Set Up Mac App Store Purchases

Apps bought using your Apple ID may be installed and reinstalled in many ways.

App Store purchases are tied to your Apple ID and cannot be transferred. Check-in with the same Apple ID when you buy an iPhone, iPad, or Mac so you can access your purchases and upgrades on this computer.

Purchased applications may be installed on another device.

Your Apple ID allows you to download and use apps across all of your devices.

1. Login to your Mac App Store account by clicking your name or Sign In if necessary.
2. Select the purchased app and hit the Download option.

   A download's progress indicator shows its pace when hovered over.

Purchased applications from one device may be downloaded to another automatically.

1. Select App Store > Settings in the Mac App Store menu.

80

2. Tap the option to "Automatically download apps purchased on other devices."

Reinstall Your Software

If you removed or deleted an app that you paid for using your Apple ID, you may install it again.

1. To access your account in the Mac App Store, click your name, or Sign In if you haven't already.
2. To reinstall a paid app, just find it and hit the download button again.

You may also install software by putting it on a disk or downloading it from the internet.

Application Installation, And Removal

Macintosh application download, installation, and removal

Apps may be installed from a disk or downloaded from the internet. You can uninstall an app if you decide you no longer need it.

Do any of the following to install software on your Mac:

- To run an internet-downloaded program, double-click the disk image or package file (open box) in the Downloads folder. Open the installer if it doesn't open automatically and follow the onscreen instructions.

- If you use disc-based software, put it into a built-in or connected optical drive on your Mac.

Remove software
Apps installed over the internet or a disk may be uninstalled.

1. Select Applications from the Finder's sidebar by clicking the Finder icon in the Dock.
2. Pick one of the options below:
   - To locate an uninstaller for a program that is stored in a folder, open the folder containing the program. If a button labeled "Uninstall [App]" or "[App] Uninstaller" appears, double-click it and then proceed as directed.
   - To uninstall a program that isn't at a specific location or doesn't have an uninstaller: The program may be deleted by dragging it from the Applications folder to the Trash can (located at the far right of the Dock).

The next time you or the Finder empties the Trash, the software will be deleted permanently from your Mac. Your previously-created files inside the program may no longer be accessible. Recover the app from the Trash before you empty it in case you change your mind and wish to retain it. Choose File > Put Back after selecting the program in the Trash.

Launchpad is where you go to remove purchased applications from the App Store.

Make Use Of A Mac For Your Document

You can make just about anything, from reports and essays to spreadsheets and financial charts to presentations and slideshows, using tools from the Mac App Store or built into macOS itself, including Pages and TextEdit.

There's a Pages file up there.

A useful trick while working with an app like Pages or TextEdit is to choose Help from the menu bar and then consult the program's user guide if you have any queries.

Make Some Paperwork

1. Launch a document-making program on your Mac.
   You can use TextEdit to create a text, rich text, or HTML document, for instance.
2. Select File > New or New Document in the Open window.

Apple's programs for word processing, spreadsheets, presentations, and more are standard on many Mac computers.

- Create everything from a letter or report to a flier or poster with Pages. Create professional-looking documents quickly and easily using Pages' numerous available templates.
- Math: Use spreadsheet software to compile and display your numerical data. You may add your own formulae, charts, photos, and more to a base document that you can then tweak in any way you wish.

- Create engaging presentations using Keynote and add media, charts, animations to slides, and more to your presentation.

Pages, Numbers, and Keynote may be downloaded from the Mac App Store if you don't already have them.

They may also be accessed on iCloud.com and downloaded on your iOS or iPadOS device from the App Store.

Layout Paperwork

On a Mac, you can format and edit text in documents using several different tools and methods:

- Format > Show Fonts, Format > Font > Show Fonts, and Format > Style let you modify a document's fonts and styles.
- To modify the document's color scheme, choose Format > Show Colors or Format > Font > Show Colors from the menu bar.
- Put in special characters like those with accents or diacritics if you need to.
- Spell check: most modern applications include built-in spellchecking and correction features. These capabilities may be disabled or replaced using other settings.

- To make sure you're using the correct terminology, highlight the text in question, right-click with Control, and choose Look Up.
- To translate text, highlight the passage you want to translate, Control-click it, and then pick Translate from the context menu that appears.

Put away paperwork
While you work, many Mac programs will automatically save your files. A document may be saved at any moment.

- To save a document, choose File > Save from the menu bar, give the file a name, and specify where you want to store it (you can see other options by clicking the down arrow button).

  Add tags to your document before saving it to make it more searchable. If you have iCloud Drive enabled on your computer and iOS/iPadOS device, you may be able to store your document there and access it from any of your devices.

- Rename the file before saving it: Select File > Save As in a document, and then give the file a new name. If Save As isn't visible, try pressing and holding the Option key while selecting File from the menu bar.

- Duplicate a file: Use File > Duplicate or File > Save As in a document to make a copy.

You may also merge numerous files into one PDF after saving a document as a PDF.

Read Files On A Mac

Double-clicking a file's icon on the desktop launches it immediately.

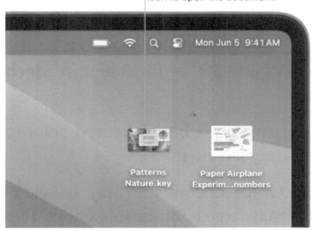

A desktop Numbers document.

There are additional methods to access files on a Mac besides clicking on their icons on the desktop.

- To open a file, just double-click its listing in the search results after selecting Spotlight from the menu bar and typing the file's name into the search box.

- Select the Apple menu > Recent Items > the document you were working on most recently.
- Launch the program that works best with your file, and then either choose File > Open or use the Open dialog to pick your file. Some programs allow you to quickly access previously used files by selecting File > Open Recent.
- To open the Finder, choose it from the Dock. Double-click the file's icon or name in the Finder's sidebar, then choose Recents, iCloud Drive, Documents, or the folder in which the file resides.

iCloud Drive must be configured before any files can be accessed via it.

Microsoft Office documents may be viewed on a Mac. You may access Microsoft Office files (Word documents, Excel spreadsheets, and PowerPoint presentations) by using the Pages software, Numbers for accessing Excel files, and Keynote for accessing PowerPoint slides. Pages, Numbers, and Keynote may be downloaded from the Mac App Store if you don't already have them.

Make Notes In Mac Documents

PDFs and photos may be annotated, signed, drawn on, cropped, and rotated using the Mac's Markup feature. With Continuity Markup and a nearby iPhone or iPad, you can annotate the file on the go, even with Apple Pencil on iPad, and see the changes reflected in real-time on your Mac.

You may utilize Continuity Markup on an iOS device by clicking the button in the Markup window, which displays a picture of the Markup toolbar.

Both Wi-Fi and Bluetooth® must be enabled and your hardware must be compatible for Continuity features to work.

1. When using Quick Look on your Mac, pick the Markup tool. Markup may also be selected from the Quick Actions menu.

   Apps like Mail, Notes, TextEdit, and Photos all support annotations.

2. To annotate a photo or PDF file on your Mac, use the following applications.

   The accessible tools change based on the data format being worked with. If you have an iOS device handy, such as an iPhone or iPad, you may utilize Continuity Markup to make notes on the document.

   You may undo your edits and start again if you're unhappy with the results.

   The Option key may be held down while dragging to create a copy of a shape, text, or signature; the yellow guidelines can be used to ensure perfect alignment. If you've made changes and decided you don't like them, you may undo them by selecting Revert.

Tool	Description
Sketch	Sketch a shape using a single stroke. If your drawing is recognized as a standard shape, it's replaced by that shape; to use your drawing instead, choose it from the palette that's shown.
Draw	Draw a shape using a single stroke. Press your finger more firmly on the trackpad to draw with a heavier, darker line. This tool appears only on computers with a Force Touch trackpad.
Shapes	Click a shape, and then drag it where you want. To resize the shape, use the blue handles. If it has green handles, use them to alter the shape. You can zoom and highlight shapes using these tools:

- *Loupe* : Drag the loupe to the area you want to magnify. To increase or decrease the magnification, drag the green handle; drag the blue handle to change the loupe size.

  To further magnify an area, you can create additional loupes and stack them, using the yellow guides to align them.

- *Highlight* : Drag the highlight where you want. To resize it, use the blue handles.

91

Text	Type your text, and then drag the text box where you wa
Highlight Selection	Highlight selected text.
Sign	If signatures are listed, click one, and then drag it where you want. To resize it, use the blue handles.

To create a new signature, click the Sign tool, click Creat Signature if shown, then click how you want to create yo signature:

- *Use a trackpad:* Click Trackpad, click the text when asked, sign your name on the trackpad using your finger, press any key when you're finished, then click done. If you don't like the results, click Clear, and th try again.

  If your trackpad supports it, press your finger more firmly on the trackpad to sign with a heavier, darker line.

- *Use your Mac computer's built-in camera:* Click Camera, hold your signature (on white paper) facing camera so that your signature is level with the blue li in the window. When your signature appears in the window, click done. If you don't like the results, click Clear, and then try again.

- *Use your iPhone or iPad:* Click Select Device to choo a device (if more than one is available). On your devi use your finger or Apple Pencil (on iPad) to sign your name. If you don't like the results, tap Clear, and the try again. When you're ready, tap done.

  If you use VoiceOver, you can add a description of a signature when you create one. This is especially use if you create multiple signatures and need to distingu between them to ensure you use the intended signatu

92

Before you click or tap Done, click the Description pop-up menu, then choose a description, such as Initials, or choose Custom to create your own description. When you're ready to sign a PDF document, navigate the list of signatures using VoiceOver. When you hear the description of the signature you want to use, press VO-Space bar.

Shape Style ≡ — Change the thickness and type of lines used in a shape, and add a shadow.

Border Color ☐ — Change the color of the lines used in a shape.

Fill Color ◩ — Change the color that's used inside a shape.

Text Style Aa — Change the font or the font style and color.

Rotate Left ☐ or Rotate Right ☐ — Click ☐ to rotate the item to the left. Continue clicking to keep rotating.

To rotate the item to the right, press and hold the Option key, then click ☐ until you're done rotating the item.

Crop ⊓ — Hide part of an item. Drag the corner handles until just the area you want to keep is shown within the frame's border. You can also drag the frame to reposition it. When you're ready, click Crop.

Image — Enter, view, or edit a description of an image. (The tool is

93

Description 💬	highlighted when an image has a description.)
	Image descriptions can be read by screen readers and are useful for anyone who has difficulty seeing images online. For example, if you use VoiceOver, you can press the VoiceOver command VO-Shift-L to hear a description of the image in the VoiceOver cursor.
Annotate 📱, 📱 , 🔄 (Continuity Markup)	Annotate the item by sketching or drawing on it using your nearby iPhone 📱 or iPad 📱. If both devices are nearby, click Annotate 🔄, then choose a device. The tool may appear highlighted to show your device is connected. To disconnect your device without using it, click the tool again.
	When you annotate items on your iPad, you can use Apple Pencil.
	To switch between your markup and the iPad Home Screen, swipe up from the bottom of your iPad with one finger. To return to your markup, swipe up from the bottom with one
	finger to show the iPad Dock, then tap the Sidecar icon 📱. When you're done with the markup, tap Done.

3. When you're done, just hit the Finish button.

   Once you shut a Quick Look or Quick Actions window, any changes you made to its contents are permanently committed.

Create A Single PDF From Many Mac Files

From your computer's desktop or a Finder window, you may easily merge numerous documents into a single PDF.

1. To launch Finder, click the Finder icon on the Dock.
2. Choose the documents you want to merge into a single PDF.

   You may also choose files from your computer's desktop.

   The PDF will reflect the selected files in the same order as they appeared in the list.

3. Choose Quick Actions > Create PDF by control-clicking the chosen files.

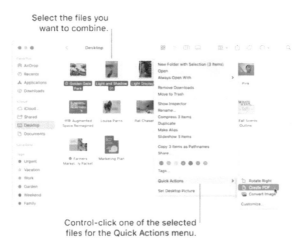

Select the files you want to combine.

Control-click one of the selected files for the Quick Actions menu.

There are now three files selected in the active Finder window, and the Create PDF option is underlined in the Quick Actions menu.

If you pick a file that sounds close to the one you want, a new file will be produced automatically.

After selecting the desired files in the Finder, you may click the Create PDF button on the window's Preview tab. Select View > Show Preview if the right-hand Preview window is hidden.

Use Stacks To Organize Your Files

When working on a Mac, use stacks to organize your files.

To keep your Mac's desktop looking tidy, you may use a feature called "desktop stacks." When a file is saved on the desktop, it is automatically filed in the correct folder.

A Macintosh computer's desktop is organized into four columns, one each for text files, pictures, slideshows, and spreadsheets.

Start Your Computer Stacks

- Click the desktop, then choose View > Use Stacks (or press Control-Command-0) to activate stacks on your Mac. Control-clicking the desktop and selecting Use Stacks is another option.

Documents may be viewed in a desktop stack.

- Mac users may swipe left or right on the stack using two fingers on the touchpad or one on a Magic Mouse.

Adjust the size of a group of desktop icons

Perform any of the following on your Mac:

- To open a stack, just click on the icon. Double-clicking an item in the extended stack will launch it.
- For each layer, look for a Down Arrow button to collapse it.

Modify the arrangement of files on your desktop.

Stacks may be organized in several different ways, including by file type (such as photos or PDFs), by date (when the item was last accessed or produced), or by Finder tags.

- To group stacks on a Mac, click the desktop, then choose View > Group Stacks By. To do the latter, right-click anywhere on the desktop and choose Group Stacks By.

Modify The Way Desktop Icons Look

You may modify the size of the icons, the distance between them, the placement of the labels, and the orientation of the labels, among other things.

- To modify your Mac's display settings, click the desktop, then choose View > Show View Options. Or Control-click the desktop, select Show View choices, then change choices.

The Dock supports stacking folders for easier navigation.

Create Folders To Store Documents

Files, media, programs, and anything else on your Mac may be found in their folders. You can stay on top of your growing mountain of paperwork, software downloads, and other tasks by creating new folders for each.

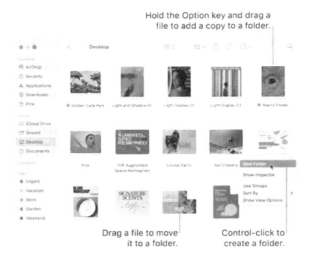

Hold the Option key and drag a
file to add a copy to a folder.

Drag a file to move
it to a folder.

Control-click to
create a folder.

Files and folders are shown in a Finder window. The New Folder option from the quick menu is highlighted.

Set Up A File System

1. Open a Finder window by clicking the Finder icon on the Dock, then go to the location where you wish to create the folder.

   If you'd rather make the folder on your computer's desktop, you may do so by clicking there.

2. Select New Folder from the File menu, or use Shift-Command-N.

   If the option to create a new folder is grayed out, you won't be able to do so at the present location.

3. Name the folder and hit Return to save it.

Transfer File To The Folder

1. To launch Finder, click the Finder icon on the Dock.
2. Take any of these actions:
   - To place anything in a folder, just drag it there.
   - Collect a few things and file them away: Drag and drop the selected item inside the folder.

     To the folder goes everything that was chosen.

   - File the contents of a window: Drag the icon that appears to the left of the window's title into the desired folder.

     If you press and hold the Shift key while pointing to the title area, the corresponding icon will show instantly. If you don't want to wait for the icon to appear, you can alternatively drag the window's title to the folder.

   - You should leave something where it is and duplicate it for safekeeping: Choose the object, hold the Option key down, and then drag it to the appropriate folder.
   - Leave anything where it is and create a new folder alias for it: To create an alias, you may either press and hold the Option and

Command keys or just drag the object to the appropriate folder.

- Create a duplicate of a file in the same directory: Choose File > Duplicate or press Command-D to duplicate the item you've selected.
- Transfer data from one disk to another. Simply drop the files onto the disk.
- Drag the files to the disk while holding down the Command key.

Create a new folder in which to store several objects quickly.

Making a new folder on your computer's desktop or in a Finder window is a simple process.

1. Select the objects you'd want to collate on your Mac.
2. Choose New Folder with Selection from the menu that appears when you control-click a chosen item.
3. Name the folder and hit Return to save it.

Combining Two Similar-Named Folders

You may combine two similar folders into a single one if they exist in separate places but have the same name.

- Hold the Option key and drag a folder to where another folder of the same name already exists on your Mac. Merge the two documents in the resulting dialogue.

  If one of the directories has content that is absent from the other folder, then the Merge option will become available. Both Stop and Replace are your sole choices if the directories include files with the same name but different extensions.

Using a Smart Folder, you may easily organize your files into groups with shared characteristics based on your criteria.

Chapter Four

Tag Your Files For Easy Organization

You may tag files and folders to make them simpler to locate. Whether they are stored locally on your Mac or in iCloud, you can use tags to organize and find them quickly and easily.

Control-click a file or folder to select a tag.

Control-click to rename a tag.
Click to show files and folders that have the same tag.

Opened in Finder, this window displays a selection of labeled files and folders. Tags are emphasized in the shortcut menu where you may choose from several tag colors.

104

Classify Data In Storage

Any document or directory may have many tags attached to it.

Perform any of the following on your Mac:

- To assign a tag to an open file, move the mouse over the right side of the document's title, click the down arrow, click in the Tags box, and then type in a new tag or choose one from the drop-down menu.
- Add metadata when you save a new file: Do so by selecting Save from the File menu. To add a tag, click the Tags box in the Save dialogue and type one in or choose one from the drop-down menu.
- In the Finder or on the desktop, label a file. Open the File menu and then choose the desired item. You may also Control-click the object. To add a tag, choose a color from the above Tags (its name will appear in place of Tags as you move the cursor over it) or click Tags.

  Pick the object in the Finder window, go to File > Get Info > Tags, and then type in a new tag or pick one from the drop-down menu.

Quickly add (or delete) your preferred tags by selecting a file and then pressing Control-1 through

Control-7 on your keyboard. When you're done using tags in a file, press Control-0 (zero).

Locate Tagged Items

1. To launch Finder, click the Finder icon on the Dock.
2. Take any of these actions:
   - Look for a label: Simply type the tag's color or name into the search bar and choose it from the results.
   - To see all files labeled with a certain tag, choose that tag in the Finder's sidebar.

     Select Finder > Settings > Tags, and then toggle the tags you'd want to have shown in the sidebar.

   - Sort things into categories using tags: To use Tags, choose them from the Group menu.
   - Organize data using tags: In any view, pick View > Show View Options, click the Sort By pop-up box, then choose Tags. When in List view, hover over the column header and click the checkbox labeled Tags to make it appear. To change the sort order, just click the column name again.

Untag this

Perform one of the following actions on your Mac:

- To untag an object, you must: To add tags to an object, select it using Control-click in a Finder window or right-click on the desktop. Choose the labels that you no longer desire, and then hit the Delete key.
- Get rid of labels on your Mac: Select Tags from the Finder's Settings menu. Select the tags you wish to delete, then click the delete button.

Remove unnecessary tags

1. To use tags in the Mac Finder, go to Finder > Settings.
2. Take any of these actions:
   - Check out a label on the Finder's sidebar: Put a check in the blue box to the right of the tag.
   - To alter the hue of a tag, just click the existing color and choose a new one.
   - To rename a tag, select it, then click its name and type in the new name.
   - Select the Add button to create a new label.
   - Remove a label: Click the Remove button after selecting the tag to remove it.
   - Put a label on the quick-access toolbar: Simply change one tag in your favorites with another by selecting it in the list and dragging it over it. The context menu that displays when you

Control-click a file allows for up to seven labels to be selected.

- Delete a label from the list: Simply slide the tag away from the Favorite Tags box until the X appears.

Use The Mac's Time Machine

Time Machine is a Macintosh's built-in backup system.

Apps, music, photographs, and documents that you've downloaded and installed in addition to macOS may be backed up using Time Machine. Time Machine will back up your Mac on an hourly, daily, and weekly basis when it is enabled.

Even if your backup drive is disconnected, Time Machine will still create local snapshots that may be used to restore data to a prior version. These copies are made every hour and kept for as long as possible, up to 24 hours (or until the disk space is required). Only drives formatted with Apple's File System (APFS) may be used to make local snapshots.

Click arrows to navigate
through backups.

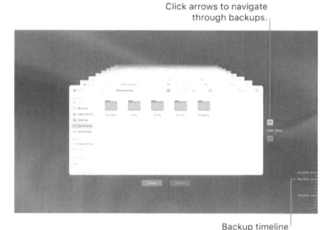

Backup timeline

Time Machine may be used to restore files that have been deleted or altered by mistake.

Multiple Finder windows, each representing a backup, are layered in the Time Machine window and may be navigated using the arrows at the top. To choose the files you want to recover, use the arrows and backup timeline on the right.

You should still back up your data somewhere other than your internal disk, such as an external hard drive, a disk on your network, or a Time Capsule, even if Time Machine produces local snapshots on PCs utilizing APFS. That way, if something ever happens to your internal drive or your Mac, you may restore your complete system to another Mac.

1. Simply plug up your external hard drive to your Mac and power it on.

   If you generate a backup on macOS 12 or later, you can only restore it to a Mac on macOS 11 or later.

2. Pick one of the options below:
   - From the "Time Machine can back up your Mac" window, create a disk: You'll be asked whether you want to utilize the disk to back up your Mac if you don't already have a Time Machine backup set up. To utilize this drive as a backup disk with Time Machine, hover over the resulting window, click Options, and then choose Set Up. (If you choose Close, Time Machine will shut down and the drive will connect as a standard disk.)
   - Create a Time Machine disk configuration: To access the Time Machine settings, choose the corresponding menu item from the main menu.

   To access Time Machine if it isn't already there, choose it from the Apple menu's System Preferences. Select "Show in Menu Bar" from the drop-down menu next to Time Machine after clicking Control Center in the sidebar.

3. When prompted, choose Add Backup Disk or tap the Add button.

   Whether or not you have a backup drive set up determines which choice you see.

Time Machine does not save any of the pre-installed programs or system data that are part of macOS.

Retrieve Mac Time Machine Backups

When you use Time Machine to back up your Mac's contents, you may effortlessly restore deleted items or revert to a previous version of a file.

1. Launch the application on your Mac that contains the file you want to restore.

   If you have deleted a file from your Documents folder and need to get it back, you may do so by opening that folder.

   If you can't find anything on your desktop, there's no need to bring up a new window.

2. To access Time Machine (located in the Other folder), launch Launchpad. While your Mac is establishing a connection to the backup drive, you may see a notice.

3. You may go through local snapshots and backups by using the arrows and the timeline.

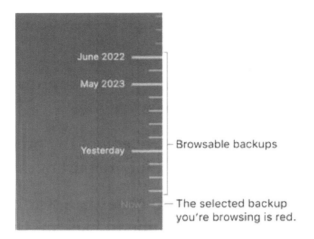

June 2022

May 2023

Yesterday — Browsable backups

Now — The selected backup
you're browsing is red.

*Tick marks in the backup timeline. When viewing a
backup, a red checkmark will appear.*

A backup that is still loading or verifying on the
backup drive will be indicated by a pulsating light
to a semi-dark gray tick mark.

4. Select the things (folders or the whole disk) you
   want to restore, and then click the Restore
   button.

   When something is restored, it goes back to
   where it was before. If anything was previously
   stored in the Documents folder, for instance, it
   will be moved back there.

To access older versions of files stored in Time
Machine, you may use File > Revert To > Browse All
Versions in many programs.

Use iCloud Drive and iCloud Photos to back up all of your important files to the cloud.

Change Your Mac's Settings

To personalize your Mac, you may alter its system settings. You may alter the wallpaper, set a bright or dark theme, and more.

Choose options on the right.

Click a setting in the sidebar.

Click for more information.

Appearance choices are on the right of the System Settings window, with Appearance chosen in the left sidebar.

Your Mac's settings are where all the options live. The Accent color and Highlight color pickers, for instance, may be found under the Appearance menu.

1. Choose Apple menu > System Settings or double-click the System Settings icon in the Dock.
2. Select a configuration by clicking on it.
   Settings are presented in the sidebar and may change based on your Mac and the programs you've installed.
3. Modify a setting.

There is often a "Help" option at the bottom of most menus that explains what each setting does.

The System Settings icon in the Dock will be badged in red if further action is required. If you haven't finished setting up iCloud, for instance, a badge will show on the corresponding icon in the Dock; clicking the icon will bring up the settings so you can finish the process.

Apps like Mail and Safari have settings that can be accessed by opening the program, clicking the app's name in the menu bar, and selecting Settings. Some applications don't allow for customization.

Alter The Desktop Background On Your Mac

The desktop background image is customizable. Choose from several photographs or colors offered by Apple, or use your images.

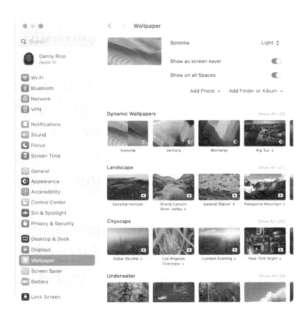

Sonoma Dynamic Wallpaper (Light) is chosen on the right side of the System Settings window. The Wallpaper settings tab in the left sidebar has been activated.

To change your wallpaper, just drag a picture from your computer's desktop or a folder into the wallpaper's thumbnail.

1. To change the wallpaper on your Mac, choose Apple > System Preferences from the menu bar. (You may have to scroll down a little.)
2. Choose a background from one of the following groups:
   - Select photos using Add Photo/Add Folder or Album.
   - Depending on the time of day where you currently are, a dynamic wallpaper will lighten or darken the background picture.
   - These still photographs reveal breathtaking landscapes, cities, underwater scenes, and the Earth from above.
   - The time between each new still picture is customizable in Shuffle Aerials.
   - These photographs depict works of artistic imagination.
   - Background colors may be set using these palettes.
3. Modify the wallpaper to your liking.

   The wallpaper you choose will determine the available options. To provide only one example:

   - Use the wallpaper's still aerial to power a slow-motion aerial screen saver.
   - You may customize the rotation frequency of your aerials.

- Dynamic Wallpaper offers both bright and dark static wallpaper options.
- Put your spin on it.

You may change your wallpaper by dragging a picture from your computer's desktop or a folder and dropping it on the wallpaper settings thumbnail.

Open the Photos app, choose the image you want to use, click the Share option on the Photos toolbar, and then select Set Wallpaper.

You may also make your desktop background an image from the internet. To set the picture as your desktop wallpaper, right-click it in the browser window while holding down the Control key.

Mac Widget Creation And Modification

You may monitor your schedule, preferred gadgets, the weather, news, and more by installing widgets in the Mac's Notification Center or on the desktop.

Drag widgets anywhere on the desktop.

Drag widgets to the upper-right corner of the desktop to add them to Notification Center.

Widget categories

The categories of widgets are shown on the left side of the widget browser.

Click the time and date in the menu bar or use two fingers to swipe left from the right edge of the trackpad to access the Notification Center. You may dismiss it by clicking anywhere in your work area.

You may reveal the widgets on your desktop by clicking the wallpaper if they are obscured by other windows.

The "Click the wallpaper to reveal desktop" feature may be toggled off under Desktop & Dock if you prefer that your open windows remain put when you click the desktop. The Stage Manager windows may be minimized by clicking the desktop.

118

Embellish Your Desktop With Widgets

1. To edit the wallpaper widgets on your Mac, use Control-click on the background.
2. You may look for a widget in the widget browser. Or you may browse the widgets by category, such as "Clock," by clicking on that category.
3. Set the location of a desktop widget mechanically. Choose the widget you want to use and click its "Add" button.
   - Place a desktop widget where you want it by hand. To reposition the widget on the desktop, just drag it there.
   - The new widget may be moved to a different spot on the desktop by simply dragging it there. Click the new widget's Remove button if you decide you don't want it.
4. When you're done customizing your widgets, choose Done from the widget browser's toolbar.

Boost Notification Center With Widgets

1. Launch the Notifications menu on your Mac.
2. Choose Edit Widgets from the drop-down menu in the Notification Center.
3. You may look for a widget in the widget browser. Or you may browse the widgets by category, such as "Clock," by clicking on that category.

4. The widget should be placed at the top right corner of the screen.
   - Choose the widget you want to use and click its "Add" button.
   - To alter the new widget's placement in the Notification Center, drag it up or down. Click the new widget's Remove button if you decide you don't want it.
5. When you're done customizing your widgets, choose Done from the widget browser's toolbar.

Put widgets for the iPhone on your Mac.
1. Select System Preferences from the Apple menu, and then select Desktop & Dock in the left pane. (You may have to scroll down a little.)
2. In the Widgets menu, activate "Use iPhone widgets."

Widgets created for the iPhone may now be added to the desktop or Notification Center.

Make Your Widgets
1. Click a widget using Control-click on a Mac.
2. Take any of these actions:
   - Modify the widget to display new data: Select Edit next to the relevant widget, then make the necessary adjustments. For instance, you may switch between reminder lists by clicking

the highlighted list in the List widget. When you're done, the widget will prompt you to click Done.

You can't modify the widget's display if the option to "Edit [widget name]" isn't there in the widget's context menu.

- Modify the widget's size by picking a new value from the drop-down menu.
- Take away the gizmo: Select the widget you want to get rid of and click Remove.

3. After making your widget adjustments, choose Done.

Take away desktop widgets

1. On a Mac, you may do this by clicking the wallpaper and selecting Edit Widgets.
2. To get rid of a widget, just click its Remove button.

Take away the Notification Center widgets

1. Launch the Notifications menu on your Mac.
2. Pick one of the options below:
   - To get rid of a widget, just right-click it while holding down the Control key and selecting "Remove Widget" from the context menu.

- To delete a widget, just hover the mouse cursor over it, hold down the Option key, and then click the Remove button.

Set Preferences For The Widget

1. Select System Preferences from the Apple menu, and then select Desktop & Dock in the left pane. (You may have to scroll down a little.)
2. In the sidebar, click on Widgets.
3. Select or uncheck the checkboxes next to "Show Widgets:"
   - Use the desktop to display widgets.
   - When Stage Manager is activated, the widgets should be shown.
     When this switch is off, the contents of the desktop are concealed; you may reveal them by clicking the desktop.
4. When the drop-down choice labeled "Widget style" appears, choose one of the following:
   - Automatic: Automatically transition between monochrome and full-color.
   - Display widgets only in black and white (monochrome).
   - Display widgets in their full, colorful glory.
5. Activate or deactivate the "Use iPhone widgets" option.

Put Your Mac Into Screen Saver Mode

If you want to protect your privacy while you're away from your Mac, you may use a screen saver to cover the desktop.

The Screen Saver preferences panel in the System Preferences window, with macOS Sonoma (Light) selected on the right.

Adjust Your Mac's Screen Saver

1. Select Screen Saver in the left pane of System Preferences (Apple menu > System Preferences)

123

on your Mac. (You may have to scroll down a little.)

2. Pick a screen saver from the following options:
   - macOS: These are slow-motion photos.
   - Dramatic aerial views of the Earth, the landscape, a cityscape, the ocean, and more, are all captured in slow motion.
   - You may adjust the time between each new slow-motion aerial view.
   - These unique screen savers give you the option to display a message, check out the "Word of the Day," and more.

3. Modify the settings for the screen saver.

Screen savers provide a wide range of customization options. To provide only one example:

- The screen saver's slow-motion aerial may be used to create a stationary background for your desktop.
- You may customize the rotation frequency of your aerials.
- To randomly see your pictures, choose a presentation type.

The Mac screen saver may be started and stopped.

- When your Mac has been inactive for the time you choose, the screen saver will activate. Select Apple menu > System Settings > Lock Screen to modify the amount of inactivity time before the screen saver activates. (You may have to scroll down a little.).

Set a "hot corner" to activate the screen saver by hovering the mouse over that area.

Select the Apple menu > Lock Screen to activate the screen saver.

- Pressing any key, pointing the mouse, or touching the trackpad will dismiss the screen saver and return you to the desktop.

Include A Mac User / Group

To prevent one user's customizations from interfering with another's, each Mac user should have an account. Allowing infrequent users to log in as "guests" gives them no access to the system or its contents. The Mac user accounts may be organized into groups. These actions need you to have administrator privileges on your Mac.

Insert a user
1. To access Users & Groups, choose it from the sidebar by selecting Apple menu > System

Settings on your Mac. (You may have to scroll down a little.)

2. Select a user type from the New User drop-down menu.

- An administrator is a user who can create and manage other users, install applications, and modify system settings. The new user you create when you initially set up your Mac is an administrator. Multiple admins are permitted on your Mac. You have the option of making regular users become admins as well as making brand-new ones. Do not enable a system administrator's automatic login. If you do, any unauthorized user may acquire administrative access to your Mac by just restarting it. Don't give out your Mac's administrator password or other sensitive information.

- Admin-created users are considered "standard" users. A standard user may only add new users and modify their settings; they cannot add new users or modify the settings of existing ones.

- Users with the "Sharing Only" permission may see shared files remotely but have no access to the whole machine or its settings.

The Help button in the dialogue's bottom-left corner provides further information about the settings available to each user type. You may need to adjust your File Sharing, Screen Sharing, or Remote Management settings to provide the person access to your shared files or screen.

3. Please provide the new user's complete legal name. A random account name is created for you. To use a different account name, enter it now—you can't alter it later.
4. A user's password must be entered and then re-entered for verification. To aid the user in remembering their password, add a clue.
5. Click Create User.
6. Limit the user's actions even further if you so want. You may accomplish any of the following by clicking the "Info" button next to the user's name:
   - Click the switch next to "Allow user to reset the password using Apple ID." The user must have iCloud installed on this Mac for this choice to be available. However, if FileVault is enabled and the user has chosen to change their password at startup using their Apple ID, the Guest User account will not have this choice.

- If you want to provide regular user permissions normally reserved for administrators, you may do so by activating the setting "Allow user to administer this computer."

After entering onto a Mac with Touch ID, a new user may add their fingerprint to the system.

Make A Group

A group is a collection of users who share the same roles and permissions. You can give a group access to a folder or a file, and then everyone in that group will have that access. Each of your shared folders might have its own set of permissions granted to a different group.

Group settings in the Users and Groups administration panel. There's a toggle to add or remove that person from the group to the right of their name. The bottom row of buttons consists of the OK, Cancel, Delete Group, and Help options.

1. To access Users & Groups, choose it from the sidebar by selecting Apple menu > System Settings on your Mac. (You may have to scroll down a little.)
2. Pick the plus sign beside "Add Group" (You may have to scroll down a little.)
3. From the New Group pop-up menu, name the group and click Create Group.
4. You may enable users by clicking the Info button next to a group and selecting them from the resulting list.

It may be necessary to adjust settings under File Sharing, Screen Sharing, or Remote Management so that additional users may access your files and screen.

Access Your Online Accounts

If you have an account with Exchange, Google, Yahoo, or another online service, you may utilize it in Mac applications.

In Internet Accounts settings, you may create new accounts and modify existing ones. Some programs also allow you to add internet accounts via their interfaces.

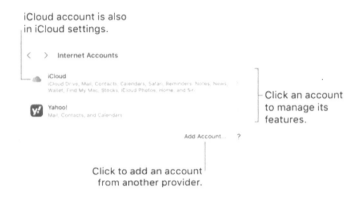

iCloud account is also in iCloud settings.

Internet Accounts

iCloud
iCloud Drive, Mail, Contacts, Calendars, Safari, Reminders, Notes, News, Wallet, Find My Mac, Stocks, iCloud Photos, Home, and Siri.

Yahoo!
Mail, Contacts, and Calendars

Click an account to manage its features.

Add Account...   ?

Click to add an account from another provider.

Configurations for online accounts that have already been set up on the Mac.

When you add an iCloud account using your Apple ID, the account details will show up in Internet Accounts as well. Both locations have access to their configuration options.

App-Based Account Creation

The Email, Contacts, and Calendar programs all provide built-in account creation wizards. Internet Accounts is where you'll find the accounts you add from these applications. You must first sign up for the service on the provider's website before adding an account via the app.

1. If you're using a Mac, you may add an account by clicking the app's name in the menu bar and selecting Add Account.
   To add an account to Mail, choose Mail > Add Account, for instance.
2. Click Continue once you've decided on an account service.

   Select Other [Type of] Account, click Continue, and then input the appropriate information to add an account from a source not mentioned, such as a mail or calendar account for your business or school. Don't guess at the account details; contact the service provider instead.

3. Type in your user ID, password, and any additional details required.
4. When creating an account that may be used by numerous applications, a dialogue box displays from which you can choose which apps will make use of the account.

Create a new account under "Internet Accounts."

You must create an account on the provider's website before adding it to Internet Accounts.

1. Go to Apple menu > System Settings on your Mac and choose Internet Accounts in the left pane of System Preferences. You may need to scroll down.
2. Select an account from the list on the right and click the provider's name to add it.
   Click Add Other Account, choose the kind of account, then enter the account data to add a mail or calendar account for your company or school from a provider not listed. If you don't know the account type or other data, contact the provider.
3. Enter your user ID, password, and any other necessary information.
4. Select which apps may utilize your account when establishing a multi-app account in the dialogue box.

Modify Your Account's Settings And Information

1. Go to Apple menu > System Settings on your Mac and choose Internet Accounts in the left pane of System Preferences. You may need to scroll down.
2. To complete one of the following, click the account on the right.
   - The account's functionality may be activated or deactivated as needed.

- To make changes to your account information, choose the Details tab. Account data such as user name or email address, description, and other information may already be shown for certain accounts, in which case the data button will not be visible.

Delete Your Online Profile

1. Select Internet Accounts in the left pane of System Preferences after selecting Apple menu > System Settings on your Mac. (You may have to scroll down a little.)
2. Select the account you no longer want to use from the list on the right, and then take the appropriate action.
   - You may delete your account and disable your services by: At the very bottom, where it says "Delete Account," click OK.
   - Switch off a certain function: Select the option by toggling the switch.

In certain cases, you may get rid of app data by deleting your account or disabling certain app functions. If you enable the functionality or re-add the account, you may be able to retrieve the lost information. If you are unsure, contact your bank.

Explore The Mac's Gallery For Shortcuts

Check out the Gallery in the Shortcuts app to find new shortcuts to add to your collection, or to understand what's possible and how certain shortcuts are made.

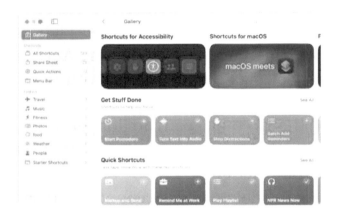

Collection of Condensed Text Documents.

View The Exhibition By Opening It

1. On the Shortcuts program on your Mac, select Gallery on the sidebar.
   The curated quick links are shown in rows labeled with their respective categories (Essentials, Morning Routine, etc.).
2. Select See All to see all of the available keyboard shortcuts.

3. To see more shortcuts for a given category, scroll the row horizontally.
4. More rows of categories will appear as you scroll up or down.

Create A Quick Link To Your Gallery

1. Click Gallery on the Shortcuts app's sidebar, then choose a shortcut to use it.

   The short-cut's details pop up.

   The shortcut collection may be rapidly added by clicking.

2. Click the More button to obtain a sneak peek of the shortcut's functions.
   Select the Done button to return to the explanation.
3. A new shortcut will be added to your collection when you choose Add Shortcut.
4. Follow the on-screen prompts for further shortcut configuration, and when finished, click Add Shortcut.

   The shortcut is added to your shortcuts collection.

Explore The Exhibits

If you need more keyboard shortcuts than the Gallery provides, you can always find more.

- To find a specific shortcut, open the Shortcuts program on your Mac, choose Gallery from the sidebar, and then use the search box at the top right.

The appropriate abridgments for your query are shown below.

Chapter Five

Make A Memoji With Messages App

A custom Memoji that reflects your character may be made with macOS 11 and later. Then, send a memo to let your friends know how you're feeling.

Select a Memoji sticker to use.

The Messages window shows a list of recent discussions on the left and a transcript on the right. Select Memoji Stickers from the Apps menu to utilize an existing Memoji or make your own.

1. Choose a thread in your Mac's Messages program.
2. Select the Apps menu to the left of the text box, then the Stickers menu item, and finally the Memoji choice.
3. Follow the on-screen prompts to create and personalize your Memoji, from the base skin tone to the accessories. Click the Add button (for your first Memoji) or the More button.
4. Put a checkmark next to Finish.

The login window also supports Memoji.

Modify Your Mac's Profile Image

Your Mac allows you to customize the image that shows in the login window. Your profile image does double duty both your Apple ID photo and your Contacts' My Card.

A user who is presently signed in (as shown by a checkmark on the user's photo) cannot have their profile picture changed. You can't alter a user's profile image until they log out and then back in again.

Click to change the user picture.

Settings for users and groups, displaying a profile image.

1. To access Users & Groups, choose it from the sidebar by selecting Apple menu > System Settings on your Mac. (You may have to scroll down a little.)

2. To access your account settings, choose the profile image to the right of your username.
   - To choose a Memoji, go to the Memoji menu, and then click the Add button. Choose a Memoji from the list and customize its appearance and stance to your liking.

- Select an emoji by going to the Emoji menu and then adding one using the plus sign. Alternately, choose an emoji from the list and then specify its appearance.
- Pick a letter combo: Select the Monogram option, pick a color for the backdrop, and then type in your initials.
- Snap a photo using your Mac's built-in camera: Select Camera. Set up your shot, then click the Camera button. If you don't like how the picture turned out, take it again.
- Pick a picture from your hard drive: View Images. Select an album and a picture inside it will load in the viewer.

  Quickly swap out photos on your Mac by dragging and dropping a new photo from the Finder onto the existing one.

- Pick one of these sample pictures: To choose an image, go to Suggestions.

3. You may change the image's appearance once you've chosen it. Take any of these actions:
   - Modify the picture's position: To reposition the image inside the circle, just drag it.
   - To zoom in or out, use the slider on the right or left.
4. A save button is available.

Modify Your Mac's Language Settings

Your Mac will default to the language of the area or nation in which it was bought, but you are free to switch it at any time. If you're fluent in French yet purchased your Mac in the States, you can change the system language to French.

App-specific language options are also available. For instance, if you have Simplified Chinese as your system language but would rather utilize a certain app in English, you may do so.

A browser like Safari will allow you to access this website in several languages. To choose a certain nation or area, scroll down to the bottom of the page and click on the appropriate entry there.

Make a language switch in the system

1. You may change your Mac's language and region settings by selecting Apple > System Settings > General > Language & Region. (You may have to scroll down a little.)
2. Choose one of the following from the drop-down menu labeled "Preferred Languages"
   - To add a language, go to the bottom-right click the Add button, and then choose a language from the drop-down menu.

There is a dividing line in this list. All menus, alerts, webpages, and other system-level elements in macOS are shown in the languages above the line. While macOS may not natively support the languages listed below, third-party programs and websites may.

A list of possible input sources is shown if you haven't previously added one for typing in the language you're adding. You may change the keyboard settings later if you forget to add an input source now.

- Swap out the default tongue: Move one language to the top of the list by dragging it there.

You'll need to restart your Mac before the changes take effect everywhere. If you want to restart your computer, click the red button labeled "Restart Now" on the right.

The interface is shown in the main language if macOS, the program, or the website supports it. If that language isn't available, the next one on the list will be used, and so on.

When entering text using characters from a script shared by more than one language, the order of the languages in the list will indicate which language(s) will be used.

If you have more than one user on your Mac and you'd want the login window to display the language you've set as the default, choose Apply to Login Window from the Settings menu. If the login window does not display the Settings menu, the default language has been selected.

You may choose the language for each app separately.

1. Select Language & Region from the sidebar after clicking General in System Preferences. (You may have to scroll down a little.)
2. In the Applications menu, choose one of the following options.
   - To choose a language for an app, click the Add button, then use the resulting pop-up options to select the desired app and language.
   - Select the application, and then select the desired language from the selection that appears.

- Take a program off the list: Make your choice and then hit the delete button. Once again, the program falls back on its default language.

To view the update, you may need to exit the app and launch it again.

Increase The Size Of Text

Increase the size of text and other Mac screen elements.

Changing the screen's resolution may make the content more legible, as can increasing the size of text and icons.

Tip: If you have difficulties locating the pointer on the screen, you can make it larger too, or quickly identify it with a shake of your mouse.

Zoom out and enlarge the screen.

You may modify your display's resolution to make everything on the screen look bigger.

1. To access the Mac's display settings, choose Apple menu > System Settings > Displays. (You may have to scroll down a little.)
2. Pick a preferred image size on the right.

   Everything on the screen will seem larger when the resolution is decreased.

Make app and system-wide text and icons larger

The font size in all of your programs, as well as on the desktop and in the sidebars, may be adjusted using the same slider.

1. Accessibility may be accessed via the Apple menu > System Preferences on a Mac. (You may have to scroll down a little.)
2. Right-click the Display menu, choose Text, and then select "Text size." (You may have to scroll down a little.)
3. If the applications you've selected are configured to "Use Preferred Reading Size," you may make the text bigger across the board by dragging the slider to the right.

Choose a new font size from the drop-down menu next to each application.

Apps with Customized in App text sizes have specific settings. System Settings changes to text size will override the app's.

Placing the pointer over text on the screen magnifies it.

Apps and system functions may have their text enlarged.

You may often customize the font size for a specific program. Desktop labels and sidebars also support resizable text.

- When reading emails, chats, and articles in applications like Mail, chats, and News, you may increase or decrease the font size by using the Command-Plus (+) or Command-Minus (-) keys.

  The font size of particular programs like Calendar, Mail, and Messages may also be adjusted under System Settings.

- To enlarge or reduce the font size in Safari while viewing a web page, press Command-Option-Plus (+) or Command-Option-Minus (-).
- When naming documents in the Finder: Choose View > Show View Options. When the "Text size" option appears, choose a new font size.

  When in Gallery mode, you cannot adjust the font size.

- Desktop decals that say: You may change the font size by right-clicking the desktop and selecting "Show View Options," followed by selecting "Text size" from the resulting menu.
- To access the Appearance panel, go to Apple > System Settings (you may need to scroll down to

find it). To make the icons in the sidebar bigger, choose "Sidebar icon size" and then "Large" from the drop-down option that appears.

Make app and system feature icons more visible by making them larger.

Items' icon sizes may be changed in the Finder, on the desktop, and in any sidebar.

- Select View > Show View Options in any Finder window to see the available view modes. Select a bigger icon size in the Icon view and List view. You may choose the size of the thumbnails shown in Gallery view.

  The size of icons cannot be adjusted in the Column view.

- To increase the size of icons on your desktop, right-click and choose "Show View Options," and then drag the "Icon size" slider to the right.
- To access the Appearance panel, go to Apple > System Settings (you may need to scroll down to find it). To make the icons in the sidebar bigger, choose "Sidebar icon size" and then "Large" from the drop-down option that appears.

Quickly zoom in or out of the screen using your keyboard, mouse, or trackpad.

Activate Focus On Mac

Focus may help you concentrate and avoid distractions when you need to get things done. Using a Focus, you may mute all incoming alerts or choose just ones you want to hear, such as those from coworkers working on a time-sensitive project. You may let others know you're busy by letting them know you've turned off alerts.

Work Focus configurations displaying available options. When in Work Focus mode, notifications from the individuals and applications listed above

will still reach you. The timed schedule that activates Work Focus is located in the center. Calendar Focus Filter is located at the bottom.

Tip: Ignore all alerts at once. Focus Control Menu, Do Not Disturb On.

Replace Or Omit A Focus

1. Select System Preferences from the Apple menu, and then select Focus in the left pane. (You may have to scroll down a little.)
2. Select an action on the right:
   - Focus on anything new by selecting it from the list offered after clicking the "Add Focus" button.
   - To create a new, personalized Focus, choose Add Focus and then Custom. Name it, give it some color, and choose an icon, then hit the OK button. You might, for instance, institute a Study Focus. Up to 10 may be made by you.
   - To edit a saved custom Focus, just choose it from the drop-down menu. Focus may have its name, color, and icon changed with a click on the icon.
   - Focuses may be deleted by selecting them from the list and then clicking the Delete Focus button.

Discarding a user-defined Focus. If you remove a Focus from the list, like Reading or Mindfulness, it won't go forever; you can always put it back.

If you update Focus on all of your Apple devices at once, any modifications you make on your Mac will automatically be sent to all of your other Apple devices.

Pick Which Alerts To Receive

A Focus may be set to only display particular types of alerts, such as those from certain individuals or applications, those that are time-sensitive, or those for incoming calls on your Mac.

Alerts from applications like Calendar only appear at certain times. Choose the toggle to enable alerts to make sure you get them.

1. Select System Preferences from the Apple menu, and then select Focus in the left pane. (You may have to scroll down a little.)
2. Focus on the right by clicking on it.
3. Select Allowed People from the Allow Notifications drop-down menu, and then proceed as follows (remember to click Done when you're done):
   - Click the drop-down option next to alerts, and then choose Allow Some People to get alerts.

Select one or more contacts to add by clicking the Add People button. You may, for instance, choose your regular gaming companions to highlight in the Gaming Focus.

Simply hover over the name of the person you want to delete and press the delete button.

- Select Silence Some People from the drop-down box next to Notifications. Select one or more contacts to add by clicking the Add People button.
Simply hover over the name of the person you want to delete and press the delete button.
- To enable incoming call alerts, open the drop-down box next to "Allow calls from," and choose an appropriate choice. On an iPhone, you may choose who gets notified when you get a call by setting it to Everyone, Allowed People Only, Contacts Only, or Favorites Only.
- When "Allow repeated calls" is on, you will get alerts from anybody who calls twice or more within three minutes.
4. Select Allowed Apps from the Allow Notifications menu, then do any of the following (ending with a click on Done when you're done):
   - Click the alerts drop-down menu and choose Allow Some Apps to enable alerts from

specific apps. To add an app or many applications, click the Add button. For example, for the job Focus, you may enable alerts just from the applications you need to accomplish your job.

You may delete an application from the list by hovering over it and selecting the Delete option.

- To turn off app alerts, you can: Select Silence Some Apps from the Notifications option that appears. To add an app or many applications, click the Add button.
  You may delete an application from the list by hovering over it and selecting the Delete option.
- Turn on alerts for things that need your immediate attention: Activate the option for "Time-sensitive notifications." (In Notifications settings, you'll want to check the box that permits applications to send you alerts.)

Whenever a gaming controller is attached to a Mac, the Gaming Focus automatically activates. Remember to add persons or applications to your notification list if you want to know when the Gaming Focus is on.

Focus may be programmed for automated on/off operation.

A Focus may be set to power on or off at certain intervals, upon entering or leaving a predetermined place, or in response to the launch of an app.

1. Select System Preferences from the Apple menu, and then select Focus in the left pane. (You may have to scroll down a little.)
2. Focus on the right by clicking on it.
3. Select Add Schedule from the Set a Schedule menu, and then perform one of the following:
   - Create a timetable that: Click Time, set a start and finish time, pick the days of the week you want the schedule to function, then click Done.

     Click the timetable you wish to modify, make your changes, and then click the Done button.

     Click the timetable, deselect Schedule at the top of the window, and then click Done to temporarily disable it.

   - Schedule activities depending on your location: Choose a location by clicking

Location, typing its name into the Search bar, and then clicking the Done button.

If you set up a location-based schedule for your Focus, it will power on when you get there and turn off when you depart.

A location-based schedule may be temporarily disabled by clicking it, toggling Automation off at the top of the window, and then clicking Done.

If you want to utilize a location, you need to make sure Location Services is turned on in your Privacy settings.

- Create a timetable using a mobile app: To install an app, go to App, type the name of the app into the Search area, and then click Done.

Focuses that are set to automatically turn on and off when certain apps are opened and closed may be used to save battery life.

Select the program whose schedule you want to disable, click Automation at the top of the window, and then click Done.

Tune the app to your needs

Focus filters allow you to modify the behavior of Calendar, Mail, Messages, and Safari while using a Focus. Tab Groups in Safari may be customized for the Work Focus, and the Work Calendar can be hidden in the Personal Focus.

1. Select System Preferences from the Apple menu, and then select Focus in the left pane. (You may have to scroll down a little.)
2. Focus on the right by clicking on it.
3. Select Add Filter under Focus Filters and then perform one of the following.
   - Create a Focus filter in Calendar by selecting the desired calendars and clicking Add.
   - Create an email filter in Focus: Select email accounts to see while this Focus is on by selecting Mail and then add.
   - To create a Messages Focus filter, pick Messages from the menu, then Filter by People List, then add.
   - Utilize Safari by setting a filter. Open Safari, click Choose next to Tab Group, choose the tab groups you want to see, turn "Open external links in your Focus Tab Group" on or off, and click Add.

You may always adjust your Focus Filter settings or temporarily disable them. To modify the Focus Filter, go to Apple > System Settings > Focus (located in the left-hand pane). Focus Filter may be toggled on and off and its parameters adjusted using the button at the top of the window. Click Done when you're done.

Select Apple menu > System Settings, then select Focus in the left-hand pane, then select Focus, then select the Focus Filter you want to delete, and finally select Delete App Filter at the bottom of the window.

Focus preferences are automatically synced throughout all of your Apple devices.

Focus settings are synced across all of your Apple devices when you use the same Apple ID on each one, and turning a Focus on or off on one device activates or deactivates it anywhere else you use that Apple ID.

1. Select System Preferences from the Apple menu, and then select Focus in the left pane. (You may have to scroll down a little.)
2. Change the setting for "Share across devices" to the right. (The setting is enabled automatically.)

Let everyone know where you are in terms of your Focus.

Your contacts won't know which Focus you're using, but you may choose to have your applications signal to them that you've muted alerts. They are at liberty to inform you otherwise if they deem it necessary.

It's a chat over Messages. If the receiver has their notification sounds muted, Messages will reflect that their message was sent in silence. The sender may send the message by clicking the "Notify Anyway" option underneath.

1. Select System Preferences from the Apple menu, and then select Focus in the left pane. (You may have to scroll down a little.)
2. To see your current concentration level, choose "Focus status."
3. Enable the option to "Share Focus status."

4. To choose which apps may broadcast your decision to mute alerts, toggle the switches next to Share From in the app's settings.

Create A Personal Screen Time Schedule

Screen Time may be activated on a Mac to reveal how much time is spent on the computer and other devices. Reports on app use, notification frequency, and total device usage are all available when Screen Time is activated.

1. To access Screen Time on a Mac, choose the Apple menu > System Settings. (You may have to scroll down a little.)
2. To choose yourself as a parent or guardian in a Family Sharing group, use the corresponding pop-up menu on the right.
3. Select App & Website Activity, and then activate it by clicking the corresponding button.
4. To enable any of the following features, use the back button, scroll down, and then click the toggle button.
   - Extensive device-sharing: To include time spent on other devices using the same Apple ID in Screen Time reports, enable this setting. You need to be logged in with your Apple ID to use this feature.

- To prevent unauthorized changes to your Screen Time limitations and settings, you may lock them by activating this option.

  If the family member already has an administrator account, you will be requested to downgrade it.

5. In addition, Screen Time allows you to accomplish the following:

   View your app and device activity by selecting App & Website Activity, Notifications, or Pickups.

   - Select Downtime to arrange maintenance.
   - Select App Limits to restrict the use of applications and websites to a specific time each day.
   - To choose programs that may be used at any time, select Always Allowed.
   - To be warned when holding a device too near, click Screen Distance.
   - Click Communication limitations, then establish communication limitations.
   - Select Sensitive Content Check under Communication Safety.

- To limit access to certain material or personal information, choose material and privacy.

Enter Text By Voice On Your Mac

Whenever you can input text, you may use Dictation to speak it instead.

If you have a Mac powered by Apple A9 or later, Dictation requests in supported languages are handled locally on your device without an active internet connection. Dictated text may be communicated to the search provider when using voice dictation in a search field. In addition, there is no word limit on the length of the text you may dictate. Dictation may be turned off manually, or it will switch off after 30 seconds if no voice is recognized.

Your dictated words are transferred to Apple for processing when using an Intel-based Mac or a language that doesn't allow on-device dictation.

Use Voice Control if you want to dictate text and navigate your Mac without touching the keyboard or trackpad.

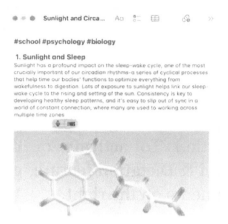

1. Sunlight and Sleep
Sunlight has a profound impact on the sleep-wake cycle, one of the most crucially important of our circadian rhythms—a series of cyclical processes that help time our bodies' functions to optimize everything from wakefulness to digestion. Lots of exposure to sunlight helps link our sleep-wake cycle to the rising and setting of the sun. Consistency is key to developing healthy sleep patterns, and it's easy to slip out of sync in a world of constant connection, where many are used to working across multiple time zones.

Dictation software is shown with dictation in a note.

Launch Dictation

1. Select System Preferences from the Apple menu, and then select Keyboard in the left pane. (You may have to scroll down a little.)
2. To activate dictation, choose it from the menu on the right. If a window pops up, choose Enable to proceed.
3. You may do one of the following when prompted to enhance Siri or Dictation:
   - Disseminate recorded audio: If you want Apple to keep recordings of your Mac's Siri and Dictation conversations, you may do so by selecting Share Audio Recordings. A piece of saved audio might be reviewed by Apple.

- Don't talk about the podcast you heard: Please do not proceed at this time.

Select Apple menu > System Settings > Privacy & Security if you decide you wish to start or stop sharing audio recordings. (You may have to scroll down a little.) To activate or deactivate the Improve Siri & Dictation feature, go to Analytics & Improvements on the right.

You may remove the audio conversations at any time since they are tied to a unique random identifier and are older than six months.

4. To change the language you're using to dictate, go to the Languages settings and click the Edit option. (Select a language if you no longer need it.)

Provide A Script

1. The dictation text will show at the insertion location in the program on your Mac.
2. If your keyboard has a function key row with a Microphone key, you may press it to begin dictating, or you can go to Edit > Start Dictation. To begin Dictation, press and release the Microphone key; to activate Siri (Siri must be enabled), press and hold the Microphone key.

3. Dictate text after hearing the Mac's ready tone or seeing the microphone sign above or below the cursor.
4. If your Mac has Apple silicon, you can dictate while typing. Writers lose the microphone icon, but when they stop typing, it reappears and they may dictate again.
5. Simple formatting tasks, including adding emojis or punctuation marks, may be done using:
   - Use the emoji's name, such as "heart emoji" or "car emoji."
   - Declare the punctuation mark or "exclamation mark."
   - Simply stating "new line" will create a new line, whereas stating "new paragraph" will create a new paragraph. When you finish dictating, a new line or paragraph will be created.

In supported languages, Dictation automatically adds commas, periods, and question marks for you as you dictate. Select Keyboard in the left pane of System Settings (accessible via the Apple menu) to disable the capability. (You may have to scroll down a little.) Select Dictation from the menu on the right, and then off Auto-punctuation.

6. If you have Dictation set up for more than one language and wish to switch languages mid-dictation, you may do so by clicking the language adjacent to the microphone or by pressing the Globe key.

7. When you're finished, use the Escape key or the Dictation shortcut. If no voice is recognized for 30 seconds, dictation will end automatically.

Unintended meanings are highlighted in blue letters. It's possible, for instance, to accidentally obtain the result "flour" while you are looking for a "flower." To change the highlighted word to anything else, click it. You may either enter the appropriate text or dictate it.

Configure The Keyboard Shortcut For Dictation

Select a predefined keyboard shortcut, or make your own, for use with Dictation.

If the Microphone key is present on your keyboard's function key row, you may use it to initiate Dictation without resorting to the shortcut.

1. Select System Preferences from the Apple menu, and then select Keyboard in the left pane. (You may have to scroll down a little.)

2. To launch Dictation using a custom shortcut, choose it from the pop-up menu next to Shortcut, located under Dictation on the right.

   Select "Customize," then use the keys you wish to assign to the action if they aren't already in the list. Pressing Option-Z is one such example.

The "Press fn key to" or "Press the Globe key to" option in Keyboard settings may automatically change when you choose a Dictation keyboard shortcut. For the Keyboard settings option to become Start Dictation (Press Fn (Function) Key Twice), for instance, you must first choose Press Fn (Function) Key Twice as the Dictation Shortcut.

Click the "Help" button inside the Keyboard settings for further assistance with the available choices.

Swap Out The Dictation Microphone

In the Keyboard preferences, you can see which microphone your Mac is using to take dictation.

1. Select System Preferences from the Apple menu, and then select Keyboard in the left pane. (You may have to scroll down a little.)
2. Select the microphone you wish to use for Dictation by clicking the drop-down arrow next

to "Microphone source" under Dictation on the right.

When you choose Automatic, your Mac will pay attention to the audio input it believes you'll most often use for Dictation.

Disable Dictation
1. Select System Preferences from the Apple menu, and then select Keyboard in the left pane. (You may have to scroll down a little.)
2. To disable dictation, choose it from the menu on the right.

Use Mac Mail To Send An Email
You may compose emails, store them as drafts, and send them at a later time.

The ability to send emails using the Mail app requires the addition of at least one email account.

Email It Over
1. To compose a new email in Mac Mail, choose New Message from the menu bar.
2. To provide the recipient's email address, click the To field's corresponding button.
   You may preserve the privacy of your receivers by hiding their email addresses in the Contacts app,

or you can send an email to many addresses at once.

3. Fill up the Subject area with your email's topic.
4. Simply compose your message and click the Send button underneath the subject line.

Email allows you to send photographs and documents as attachments in addition to the plain text you write.

5. A send button should be clicked.

Keep An Unfinished Draft

1. Make sure you're seeing the message you wish to archive in Mac Mail.
2. To save your work, choose File > Save.

You may simply dismiss the notification box and save your changes using the Save As prompt that displays.

When you wish to return to your draft, you may locate it in the Drafts inbox (via the Favorites bar or the Mail sidebar).

Set Up A Future Email

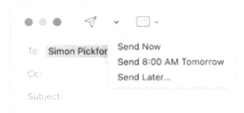

There's a drop-down list on the message pane with choices like "Send Now," "Send 8:00 AM Tomorrow," and "Send Later" for when you want to send the email.

Choose one of the following actions in the Mac's Mail app:

- Time your email: To send at a specific time or a later date, select the option to do so from the menu that appears when you click the Send button.
  The message is saved in the Mail sidebar's Send Later inbox.
- Adjust the time an email is sent: To edit an email, open it by double-clicking on it in the Send Later folder and then clicking the Edit button.
- Once you've made your selection, you can delete the message from your Send Later inbox.

Using A Mac Rely Messages

Macintosh messages don't have to be dull. Once your Mac is all setup, you can send messages to individuals, groups, and businesses with the ability to include text, photos, animated effects, and more. There are many avenues open to you for self-expression:

- Tapbacks.
- Images and film
- Images, scans, and sketches (made on an iPad or iPhone).
- Images and stickers.
- Sound recordings.
- Use message effects.

Tapback | Image | Memoji

Click the Apps button to add photos, videos, #images, stickers, and message effects.

Live Sticker

The Messages window shows a list of recent discussions on the left and a transcript on the right. A Tapback is featured above a pinned conversation on the left, a picture and Memoji on the right, and a Live Sticker in the bottom right corner of the transcript. To insert media (photos, videos, #images, stickers, and message effects), select the Apps tab at the window's footer and click the appropriate app.

1. To compose a new message in Messages (or to use the Touch Bar), click the Compose button.
2. Enter the recipient's name, email address, or phone number in the To field. As you type, Messages will offer up potential recipients based

on people you've already messaged or contacts you have on your device.

The Add button next to the To input field is another option. To access an individual's email or phone number, select them from the list and click the relevant link.

If you can only send and receive messages with selected contacts, the hourglass icon will appear next to their names.

3. Just use the box down there to type your note. If they are available, you can use the autocomplete function while typing.

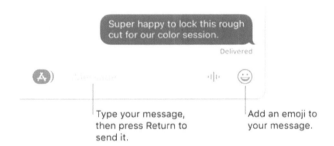

Type your message, then press Return to send it.

Add an emoji to your message.

A transcript, with the message field visible, in the Messages window.

Siri, tell Mom I'll be late by saying something like "Message Mom that I'll be late."

4. To send the message, either press Return on your keyboard or select the Send option.

If you have a Game Center account, you can use messages to invite new people to play multiplayer games with you.

Chapter Six

Make And Receive Video Calls

Use a Mac to make and receive video calls with FaceTime.

If both parties are using an iOS device, they can use FaceTime to see and hear each other. Your Mac's Wi-Fi connection is utilized for FaceTime video calls.

The brand-new FaceTime interface—either manually enters call recipients or selects them from the Suggested list.

Use Facetime For A Video Chat

1. Select New FaceTime in the FaceTime menu on your Mac.
2. Type the contact's email or phone number into the New FaceTime window to initiate a call. Pressing Return could be necessary.

   To quickly find someone who is already in your Contacts, enter their name and choose them from the Suggested list. The New FaceTime window also allows you to add people to your contact list.

3. Select FaceTime or make use of the Touch Bar.

Just say something to Siri like "FaceTime mom."

Join A Facetime Video Chat

If you're already logged into your account and have FaceTime enabled, you'll be able to take calls even if the app isn't currently open.

When a pop-up appears in the upper-right corner of your Mac, you can choose between the following actions:

• The Accept button answers an incoming call.
• Allow a video call to be received as an audio call: Select Answer as Audio by clicking the arrow to the right of the Accept button. The camera will

turn off automatically while you are on an audio or phone call.

- Take the incoming call and hang up: Just hit the Accept and Quit button.
- Click the "Decline" button to end a call.

  The decline option also includes a drop-down menu from which you can send a text message or set a reminder.

  You can block the number if it is someone you'd rather not hear from again.

Once a call has begun, additional participants can be added or a link to the call can be shared.

Turn Down A Facetime Video Chat

You can ignore a call even if FaceTime isn't open if you're signed in and the feature is activated.

When a pop-up appears in the upper-right corner of your Mac, you can choose between the following actions:

- Click the "Decline" button to end a call.

  You've let the caller know that you're currently unavailable.

  You can block the number if it is someone you'd rather not hear from again.

- To reject a call and communicate via iMessage: Click the down arrow next to Decline, choose Reply with Message, type your message, and then click Send. You and the person calling you must both be using iMessage.
- Reject a call and schedule a return call: To receive a reminder, select an appropriate time frame and then click the arrow next to Decline. A reminder will be sent to you at the appointed time; upon opening it, you can begin your call by clicking the link provided there.

Cut off a FaceTime call

Move the cursor over the call window and click Leave Call (or use the Touch Bar) to end the call.

Photo Editing On The Mac

You can easily adjust the brightness, contrast, and saturation, as well as crop and rotate images with the Photos editing tools. Photos can be copied so that modifications can be tested, and changes can be pasted to other images. A photo's edits can be rolled back if the user decides they don't like the results.

Alter A Video Or Picture

1. Choose one of the following actions in the Mac Photos app:

- To edit a photo or video, double-click its thumbnail and select Edit from the menu.
- Press Return after clicking on a preview image or video.
2. Take any of these actions:

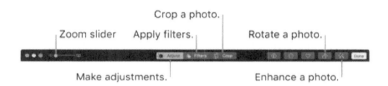

Crop a photo.
Zoom slider   Apply filters.   Rotate a photo.
Make adjustments.   Enhance a photo.

A zoom slider and options to edit, apply filters, crop, rotate, and enhance your photos are displayed in the Edit menu.

- Image magnification and reduction: The Zoom slider can be moved by clicking and dragging it.
- Make some changes: To access the tools for making modifications, select Adjust.
- Change your photo or video's look with filters: Click Filters.
- Image cropping: To see your cropping options, select Crop from the editing menu.
- To rotate an image or video 90 degrees counterclockwise, select it and then click the rotate button in the toolbar. Keep clicking until the desired orientation appears. The

image will be rotated clockwise with a single click of the Option key.

- To have your photo or video's color and contrast automatically adjusted, just click the Auto Enhance button. Use Command-Z or the Undo button to undo your most recent changes.

3. Clicking Done or pressing Return will save your changes.

Use the arrow keys to quickly navigate between tools and your current selection in the image or video editor.

Make A Photocopy

Duplicating and editing a photo or video creates different versions.

1. Choose the photo you want to copy in the Photos app on your Mac.
2. To duplicate a single image, select Image > Duplicate 1 Photo (or hit Command-D on your keyboard).

When duplicating a Live Photo, you have the option of keeping the video component or just the still image.

Examine the original and final versions of a photo or video.

The edited version of an item can be compared to the original while editing.

1. To edit a photo or video in the Mac Photos app, double-click the file to open it, and then select Edit from the menu bar.
2. To view the unaltered original, press and hold the M key or the Without Adjustments button.

   When you're ready to view the revised item, press the button or the M key again.

Click and hold to see your photo without adjustments.

Located in the top left corner of the window, next to the other controls is the Without Adjustments button.

Revisions By Cut-And-Paste

After you modify a picture or video, you may copy the adjustments that you've made and paste them on other objects. Multiple things may be updated at once by copying and pasting changes.

The settings for the retouch tool, red-eye tool, crop tool, and any third-party extensions cannot be copied and pasted.

1. To see your changes in the Photos app, double-click the object and choose Edit from the menu bar.
2. Select Image, then Edit Copies.
3. To make changes, select the item (or select several items with Command-click).
4. To edit an image by pasting its contents, choose Image > Paste Edits.

In addition, when in edit mode, you may select an item by Control-clicking it and then clicking Copy Edits or Paste Edits.

Delete Your Changes

A picture or video may have its edits undone in a flash.

Perform any of the following in the Mac Photos app:

- Cancel the most recent edit: Select Undo from the Edit menu, or use Command-Z.
- Revert to the original and erase your edits: Choose Image > Revert to Original once you've decided on a photo or movie.

Extract And Reuse Text From Images

Photos' Live Text feature makes it easy to extract and reuse text from images. The words on a roadside sign, for instance, may be copied and pasted into a message or email.

Pictured above is a For Sale sign advertising real estate, with the agent's contact information highlighted in Live Text, with a menu offering further actions such as saving the contact to Contacts, dialing the number, initiating a FaceTime conversation, sending a text message, and more.

1. Launch Photos on your Mac and choose a picture with text to see it.
2. Drag the mouse over the text you want to choose.
3. Take any of these actions:
   - Text to copy: Select what you want to copy, then right-click or press Command-C. The copied text may then be pasted into another program.
   - Read up on a topic in a dictionary: Make a selection using Control-click, then choose Look Up [text].
   - Into Translation: Select the text you want to be translated, right-click it, and select Translate [text].

     Not all languages and not all areas have access to translation.

   - Look for the article online: To use a web search engine on a selected area, Control-click the area and choose Search with.
   - Talk about what you've read: Select the text you wish to share, right-click on it, and select "Share."
   - Call the following number: To make a phone call, initiate a FaceTime video or audio call, or send a message to the selected number, use the Control-click or down arrow.

- For an email address, please: Choose to either create a new email or add the address to your Contacts by using the Control-click menu or the down arrow.
- Surf to a site: Control-click your selection or click the down arrow, then open the link in your browser or use Quick Look to examine the website details.

Create A Note In A Hurry On A Mac

No matter what you're doing on your Mac, you can always use Quick Note to scribble down thoughts and attach relevant links. While it's open, your Quick Note won't hide from view, making it simple to drag and drop data from other programs into it.

Create a Note in a Hurry

Quick Notes are simple to launch from anywhere, so you can get one going even if you're deep in another program. Pick one of the options below:

- Press and hold the Fn key (or the Globe key) and the Q key to activate the shortcut.
- Quick Note's default hot corner is the bottom right of the screen; to access this note, just move the cursor there and click.
- View with Safari.

Quick Notes may be closed by selecting the red Close button located in the note's upper left corner. Use any of the aforementioned entry points to reopen the Quick Note.

If you'd like to create a fresh Quick Note each time (rather than accessing the old one), go to Notes > Settings and uncheck "Always resume to last Quick Note."

Embed Websites in a Quick Note Using Safari

1. Access the target web page by opening it in Safari on your Mac.
2. Select New Quick Note or Add to Quick Note after clicking the Share button.

   When you return to the linked content on the site, a thumbnail of the Quick Note shows in the corner of the screen to remind you of what you noted previously.

Notes additionally allow you to include in-app and web-based link references.

Insert Safari text into a note

Selecting content from a web page and pasting it into a Quick Note is a possible action.

1. If you wish to copy and paste some text from a website into a Quick Note, open Safari on your Mac and copy the content.
2. Right-click the text and choose New Quick Note or Add to Quick Note from the menu that appears.

   The content in Safari is underlined and a link appears in the Quick Note. The highlighted text will remain even if you return to the page at a later time.

You may highlight anything by erasing the Quick Note link to Safari.

Modify a Hasty Note
Your Quick Notes show in the Quick Notes folder in the Notes app. Include tables, tags, and more with a little editing. Check out any of these options:

- Insert a table
- Label it
- Make a list
- Embedding references
- A Quick Note cannot be secured.

Use Maps To Get Instructions

You can obtain instructions for every mode of transportation you use, whether it's a car, foot, bike, or public transit. It is possible to include many stops within a driving trip. The instructions may also be sent to your mobile device, such as an iPhone, iPad, or Apple Watch, for easy access on the road.

Not all nations or areas provide directions for several stops.

Driving instructions between two points are shown on a map of the San Francisco region. The map also displays options for taking other routes.

Get Direction

1. You may perform one of the following in the Maps program on your Mac:

- Simply input your origin and destination coordinates after clicking the corresponding button in the toolbar.
- After selecting a landmark or map pin as your destination, choose Directions from the place card's menu.

  If your current location is shown, Maps will use it as your starting point; however, you may change this if you'd like. To switch the order of your beginning and finishing points, just drag the Reorder button to the left or right of a place.

  If you have someone's name and they have shared their location with you, you can search for them in Find My (not accessible in all countries or regions) and obtain directions to their address or location.

2. Choose an option: Drive, Walk, Transit, or Bike.
3. To see the set of directions for a certain route, choose it and then click the Trip Details button.

Directions for motorists might include things like:

- If you're driving an electric car, the app can show you where to plug in along the way and how much juice you have left.

- Major cities like London, Paris, and Singapore use congestion zones to manage traffic flow in congested regions. During the times when these restrictions are in place, you may find a way to avoid them.
- If you have the right license plate for one of China's cities that restricts entry to congested regions, you may find a path around or around the restricted area.

  In some urban centers, cyclists may get instructions to their destination.

4. Take any of these actions:
   - Focus on a certain procedure: Follow the on-screen prompts by clicking the corresponding button.
   - Select your desired departure or arrival time by clicking Plan for both driving and public transit options.
   - Click the Trip Details button again to hide the direction list.

Find out how to go to many places while behind the wheel.

1. You may perform one of the following in the Maps program on your Mac:

- To get directions, just hit the toolbar's directions button and plug in your origin and destination.
- After selecting your starting point (a landmark or map pin, for example), go to the Directions section of the location card.

  If your current location is shown, Maps will use it as your starting point; however, you may change this if you'd like.

2. Click the Drive button.
3. Select a previously visited place by clicking it, or enter a new destination and select it from the list that appears after clicking Add stop.
   To add more stops, just repeat the process.
4. Take any of these actions:
   - You may rearrange the order of the stops by dragging the Reorder button adjacent to a stop.
   - To make a stop change, click the stop, then pick a comparable place from the drop-down menu, or type in a location and click the search result from the list.
   - To remove a stop, hover over it and press the Delete key on your keyboard.

Get Direction Automatically

If you're using the same Apple ID on your Mac and iOS device, you may search for a route on your Mac and then open it in the Maps app on your iPhone (running iOS 16 or later) or iPad (running iPadOS 16 or later).

1. Launch the Maps app on your iOS device.
2. To access the route, go to Recents in the search card's drop-down menu.

Get walking or driving instructions sent to your Apple device.

Your other gadgets may be sent instructions or a location. (You'll need to be logged into the same Apple ID on both your Mac and your mobile device.)

Only single-stop driving routes may be shared with others.

1. To customize your route in the Maps app, just choose a place, then click Directions.
2. Select the destination device from the drop-down menu after clicking the Share button in the toolbar.
3. You may check the route on your Maps app.

Your electronic gadgets also allow you to tailor riding routes.

How Does Family Sharing Work?

Apple Music, Apple TV Plus, iCloud Plus, Apple Fitness Plus, Apple News Plus, and Apple Arcade memberships may all be shared between up to six people in the same household via Apple's Family Sharing feature. All of your family members may access and contribute to the same family picture album in iCloud, as well as share purchases from the iTunes Store, the App Store, and Apple Books. You may also use this to assist each other in finding lost gadgets.

In the family settings, you can see all the people associated with an existing account, as well as the various account types that are compatible with Family Sharing.

Family Sharing is set up by one adult (the family organizer), who may add up to five family members and decide which features they can share. When family members join, they get immediate access to the shared material.

To access Family settings, each member of the family must have an Apple ID and be logged in with that ID. A child's Apple ID and membership in the group may be set up by the organizer, a parent, or a guardian.

Only one family (adults and children) should utilize Family Sharing at a time. Only one Family Sharing group may include you at a time.

Macs running OS X 10.10 or later, iOS 8 or later, iPadOS, and Windows PCs running iCloud for Windows (Windows 7 or later needed) all support Family Sharing.

Initiate Mac Family Sharing

Family Sharing is organized by one adult who invites other adults to participate. Each family member needs an Apple ID to participate.

In the family settings, you can see all the people associated with an existing account, as well as the various account types that are compatible with Family Sharing.

1. Navigate to System Preferences in the Apple menu, then locate "[your name]" at the top of the sidebar.

   If your name doesn't display, pick "Sign in with your Apple ID," enter your Apple ID (or a Reachable At email address or phone number from Apple ID settings), and then enter your password. Get an Apple ID if you don't have one.

2. Gather the family: Follow the on-screen steps after selecting Invite People.

- Select Invite in Person if the person you want to invite is physically close by and you wish to have them input their Apple ID and password on your Mac. In any other case, you may use Mail, Messages, or AirDrop to extend the invitation.

  Your invitee will need to sign up for a new Apple ID if they don't already have one.

- Make a child's first Apple ID: Follow the prompts to set up a new account for your kid by clicking the button.

3. Follow the on-screen prompts to invite other family members to join your Family Sharing group.
4. To take any action:
   - Carry out the recommended actions: Select the Family Record button. You're presented with some tips for optimizing your Family Sharing experience. Parental restrictions, location sharing, and a recovery contact may all be set up.
   - Look for a shared subscription service: Click Subscriptions. Your available subscription services are shown. To make a subscription available to relatives and friends, click the

name of the service and then follow the on-screen instructions.

Except for iCloud+, all Apple subscriptions may be shared between up to six family members. You and your loved ones have the option of combining iCloud+ storage subscriptions or keeping your own separate storage space.

Click Apple Subscriptions or the service's name in the "Discover More" section to discover more about further Apple subscription options. Select Discover next to Subscriptions for Family in the App Store to look into further options tailored to families.

- Create a system for group buying: Select Buy Together, then Proceed, and finally Enable Buy Together. The members of your household may easily share their iTunes, App Store, and Apple Books purchases. The pooled payment method you set up will be used for all future transactions.
- To share your location with friends and family, go to Settings Location Location Sharing and toggle the switch for the people you wish to share your location with. If you want your location shared automatically with

any new family members who join later, you may set this to happen. The Find My and Messages applications provide location sharing, so family members may see each other's whereabouts. The Find My app is available on the Mac, iOS, and iPadOS platforms, as well as iCloud.com.

- To activate Ask to Buy, choose a family member's name, go to the Family Sharing settings, and then click the Ask to Buy option. Your Family Sharing group's young members will need your permission before they can make any App Store, iTunes Store, or Apple Books purchases.
- Ask to Buy has varying age requirements in different regions. The family organizer in the United States may enable Ask to Buy for any member of the family under the age of 18; by default, Ask to Buy is enabled for children under the age of 13.
- To configure Screen Time and parental controls, go to Settings > Screen Time > Open [family member's] Screen Time > and then choose the desired settings. Learn how to limit a kid's screen time here.

Limits on children's exposure to media depend on location. In the United States, anybody over the age of 18 may use Screen Time, but it must be activated by the family organizer.

To make purchases from the iTunes Store, the App Store, and Apple Books accessible to several users at once, each user must first sign in with their own Apple ID. In Family settings, everyone in the family has access to this.

How To Limit A Child's Computer Use
Family Sharing is the easiest way to set and manage a child's Screen Time. Family Sharing lets you monitor your kids' Mac, iPhone, or iPad usage from your device. Even without Family Sharing, setting up Screen Time for a child needs access to their Mac account.

Web Content Filter and Communication Safety for under-13s are activated by default to block unsuitable content online.

Screen Time settings with a kid picked from the Family Member pop-up menu and Screen Time switched on.

1. Perform one of the following actions on your Mac:
   - Family Sharing requires you to check in using your Apple ID to your Mac user account.
   - Sign in to the kid's Mac account if you're not using Family Sharing.
2. Select System Preferences (Apple menu) > Screen Time (System Preferences) > Screen Time (sidebar). (It may be necessary to scroll below.)
3. Select a kid from the drop-down option that appears if you're using Family Sharing.

4. Follow the on-screen prompts after clicking the "Set Up Screen Time For Your Child" button.
Content filters, Screen Distance, App and website Activity, Screen Time away from displays, and a 4-digit password may all be configured during setup.

5. To activate any of these features, go to Screen Time's settings and scroll down to the bottom.
   - To have information about the websites visited included in Screen Time reports, toggle the Include Website Data switch. If you don't enable this setting, Safari will only record your visits to known websites.
   - To extend your Screen Time allowance after it has expired, you may lock the Screen Time settings with a password by activating this feature.

     If the family member already has an administrator account, you will be requested to downgrade it. See Insert a user or a group.

6. In addition, Screen Time allows you to accomplish the following:
   - View your app and device activity by selecting App & Website Activity, Notifications, or Pickups.
   - Select Downtime to arrange maintenance.

- Select App Limits to restrict the use of applications and websites to a specific time each day.
- Select the Always Allowed option and then pick the applications you want to access whenever you want.
- To get notifications when you're holding your smartphone too near, go to Settings > Screen Distance.
- Select "Communication Limits" to put restrictions on your interactions.
- Select Sensitive Content Check under Communication Safety.
- To limit access to certain material or personal information, choose Material & Privacy.

Use Family Sharing To Share Purchases

Mac users may use Family Sharing to share purchases with close relatives.

When you join a Family Sharing group, you'll have instantaneous access to everyone's pooled purchases. Their purchases are always available for download on any Mac, iOS, or iPad device.

Your friends in the group will have the same access to your purchases as you will. You have the option to conceal your purchases from the rest of the group.

To set up purchase sharing, only the family organizer may do so (see Set up Family Sharing).

Check out what your loved ones have bought and share the files

The method you download purchases made by other family members differs based on the app.

- Listen online or download the MP3: To access your purchased content, launch the Music app on your Mac and choose Account > Purchased. To share your purchases with a family member, click the ellipsis (...) next to Purchased, select the person, and then click Share.
- Get app info or download: Launch the Mac App Store app and log in with your Apple ID and password. Select a relative from the "Purchased by" drop-down option and then download the desired products.
- Download or read books online: Launch Books on your Mac, then go to the Menu Bar and choose Account > View My Account. To access your family's downloads, choose them from the list under Family Purchases.

A member of the family may purchase at any time, and the organizer will be charged for it. Once an item is bought, it is added to the account of the person who made the initial purchase, and the rest of the family gets access to it. If the family organizer ever decides to end Family Sharing, everyone will retain the products they've purchased, regardless of who paid for them.

Keep a purchase secret from other members of the family

You can keep your personal iTunes, App Store, and iBooks purchases from being seen by other members of your household.

- Select Account > Purchased in the Mac Music app to hide music. To conceal material, first, choose the category it belongs to, then move the cursor over it, click the Delete option, and lastly, choose Conceal.
- To conceal applications, launch the Mac App Store application, log in, and then choose Store > Account. To conceal an app purchase, hover over the item, click the More Options option, and then choose Hide Purchase.
- Sign in to the Books program on your Mac, then choose All (or another collection) from the left

sidebar to hide the books. To conceal an item, select it, click More Options, then Remove, and finally Hide item type>.

Don't try to cover up a purchase you made.

To make your Music, App Store, and Apple Books purchases accessible to other members of your household, you may unhide them.

- We must not be afraid to hear music: Select Account > Account Settings after logging into the Music app on your Mac. Select Downloads and Purchases, then select Manage, and then select Unhide next to the relevant item.
- No more app obscuring! Launch the Mac App Store app and log in with your Apple ID and password. Select the Preferences tab. You may unhide an item by going to the Hidden Items area, clicking Manage, and then clicking Unhide.
- Put away the books: Launch Books on your Mac, then go to the Menu Bar and choose Account > View My Account. To reveal a previously hidden purchase, choose Manage Hidden Purchases, log in with your Apple ID and password, and then select Sign In.

Don't brag about what you've bought.

When you cease family sharing, they no longer have access to any of your shared purchases from the iTunes Store, the App Store, or Apple Books.

1. Select System Preferences from the Apple menu, and then Family from the left pane.
Set up Family Sharing if you don't see the Family option.
2. Select [your name], then click Purchase Sharing to disable the option to not share your purchases.

Disabling Purchase Sharing

By disabling purchase sharing for your Family Sharing group, all previously shared purchases in the iTunes Store, App Store, and Apple Books will be removed, and no further shared purchases will be possible.

The group's purchase-sharing feature can only be disabled by the family organizer.

1. Select System Preferences from the Apple menu, and then Family from the left pane.
Set up Family Sharing if you don't see the Family option.
2. Right-click Purchase Sharing, then Stop, then Stop again.

All family members' iTunes Store locations must be the same for the purchases to be shared. Changing the iTunes Store nation or region may prevent access to family members' purchases and prevent applications that were shared among family members from functioning properly after installation.

Coordinate Your Work Across Devices

You may use Continuity to coordinate your work across your various Apple devices.

Continuity allows you to utilize your Mac in tandem with your other Apple devices so that you may multitask more efficiently and easily switch between them.

An iPhone with a FaceTime call is shown next to a Mac with the Handoff indicator on the FaceTime

program icon near the right end of the Dock, indicating a handoff.

Use the same Apple ID across devices to get Continuity features. The system requirements also include having Wi-Fi and Bluetooth® enabled on your devices.

Airdrop

With AirDrop, you can instantly send files to nearby friends and family via Wi-Fi, whether it's a picture, a video, a contact, or anything else.

Mac Airplay

You may mirror the display of another Apple device to your Mac and use it to share, play, or show material.

Access and Approval with Apple Watch Automatically

Unlock your Mac with your Apple Watch, or use it to confirm authentication requests made by your Mac, without entering a password.

Rolling Camera System

If you have an iPhone or iPad handy, you can use it as a camera on your Mac, snap a photo, or scan a document, and have it show on your computer quickly.

Markup For Continuity

The Markup tools, including Apple Pencil for iPad, allow you to annotate PDFs and images on your Mac, and then send them to your iOS device for viewing and editing.

Sketch Of Continuity

Create a sketch on your nearest iOS device, then see it appear on your Mac in real-time.

Handoff

Documents, emails, and messages begun on one device may be continued and completed on another. Mail, Safari, Maps, Messages, Reminders, Calendar, Contacts, Pages, Numbers, and Keynote are just some of the applications that benefit from Handoff.

Rapid Connectivity

Not connected to Wi-Fi? Sure, no sweat. Your Mac may connect to the internet via the personal hotspot on your iPhone or iPad when they're within range of each other—no configuration is necessary. Selecting your iOS device from the Wi-Fi menu on your Mac will activate your hotspot.

Communicating Via Telephone

Don't grab your iPhone; rather, use your Mac to place and receive calls. Calls may be initiated from a wide variety of iOS applications, including

FaceTime, Contacts, Safari, Mail, Maps, and Spotlight. A pop-up alert shows whenever you get a call. To respond, just click the alert.

Sidecar

You may expand your workspace by presenting additional applications and windows when you use your iPad as a second display alongside your Mac.

In-Second Messaging System

You may use your Mac to send and receive SMS and MMS messages. When friends send you text messages, regardless of what phone they have, you may react from whatever device is nearest. Your Mac now displays all of the messages that show up on your iPhone.

Universal Clipboard

It is possible to copy material from one Apple device and paste it into another. If you're using Safari on your Mac and want to save a recipe for later, you may copy the ingredients and paste them into Notes on your iPhone.

Universal Control

You may share the same keyboard, trackpad, or linked mouse amongst several Macs and iPads when they are close to one another. You can also drag and drop material between them; for instance, you may use Apple Pencil to draw on an iPad and then transfer the image to your Mac to include it in a Keynote presentation.

Put The iPhone Camera As A Webcam

Put the strong iPhone camera and extra video effects to work on your Mac by using it as a webcam with Continuity Camera. You may use wireless networking or a wired connection (via a USB cable) to go online.

A FaceTime conversation captured with an iPhone being used as a camera on a MacBook Pro.

First things first

The following must be done before the Continuity Camera function may be used:

- Make sure you're using iOS 16 on your iPhone, and macOS 13 or later, on your computer.

  You'll need macOS 14 on your Mac and iOS 17 on your iPhone to make full use of Continuity Camera.

- Use the same Apple ID to log onto both devices.
- Enable wireless networking and Bluetooth® on both gadgets.
- Verify that your hardware can run the required software.
- Get your iPhone mounted.

Convert Your iPhone Into A Webcam
Convert your iPhone into a microphone or webcam.

1. Launch a program that can use the Mac's microphone and camera, such as FaceTime or Photo Booth.
2. You may use your iPhone's camera and microphone by selecting them in the app's settings or main menu.

When you launch Continuity on your iPhone, it will begin sending whatever is being recorded by the rear-facing camera to your Mac.

Your iPhone must be in landscape mode, immobile, and have its screen turned off to be used as a microphone on a Mac without a built-in camera. You may also connect your iPhone to your Mac via USB.

3. To take any action:
   - Slide up to unlock your iPhone or touch Pause to pause video or music.
   - To continue playing music or video, hit the side button or Sleep/Wake button on your iPhone.
   - Put down the iPhone and use it for something else: Close the program if it's running on your Mac.
   - Disconnecting your iPhone is as simple as tapping the Disconnect button and then tapping the Confirm button. Sound settings no longer include your iPhone as an input device, and applications no longer have access to its camera or microphone.

   Connect your iPhone to your Mac via USB to restore it.

Use a USB cord if you need to charge your iPhone when Continuity Camera is on.

Invoke The iPhone's Camera Instantly

Apps like FaceTime and Photo Booth on the Mac may immediately switch to utilizing the iPhone's camera as the input. Your iPhone needs to:

- Turn off the screen.
- Have a landscape stance
- Allow the camera or cameras in the back to point directly at you without obstruction.
- Not be tucked up in a pocket or laid out flat on a table
- Stand still

If you've used your iPhone as a webcam on your Mac previously, other Mac programs may also remember it as the primary camera.

Set your iPhone as the primary recording device.

Your Mac may use the iPhone's microphone by default.

1. To adjust the Mac's audio settings, choose Apple menu > System Settings > Sound. (It may be necessary to scroll below.)
2. Choose the iPhone from the list of audio inputs.

The Continuity app launches on the iPhone and begins recording sound.

Start The Video And Activate Desk View

Using your iPhone as a Mac webcam is as simple as clicking the Video button in the top menu. Studio Light reduces ambient light and highlights only your face, while Desk View provides an overhead perspective of your workspace.

If your iPhone isn't recognized as a camera or microphone,

Try the following if your iPhone isn't showing up as a camera or microphone in a given app's Sound settings.

1. Try again after plugging the USB cord into your Mac. (If a cable is already attached, remove it and reattach it.)
2. To verify, please see:
   - It seems like you're using an iPhone XR or later.
   - iOS 16 or later is installed on your iPhone.
   - You're using an OS version of Mac computers greater than or equal to 13.
   - You have enabled Continuity Camera on your iPhone by going to Settings > General > AirPlay & Handoff.
   - The Mac has been verified as a reliable computer by your iPhone.

- Both your iPhone and Mac have Wi-Fi, Bluetooth, and two-factor authentication.
- Your Apple ID is used to access both your iPhone and Mac. (Managed Apple IDs can't use this function.)
- The distance between your iPhone and Mac is less than thirty feet.
- Neither your iPhone nor your Mac are sharing their data plans with anybody else.
- The most recent version of your selected video app has been installed.

If your Mac doesn't have a built-in camera, your iPhone may be used as a camera as long as it fits all of the requirements for switching to the iPhone camera. A USB cord allows you to connect your iPhone to a Mac.

You may utilize Continuity Camera to rapidly import scanned documents or photos of adjacent objects into your Mac.

Wirelessly Transmit Media From Your Mac

AirPlay allows you to wirelessly transmit media from your Mac.

By connecting your Mac to your preferred speakers (including HomePod mini), Apple TV, and certain smart TVs via Wi-Fi, you can use AirPlay to wirelessly stream music, films, photographs, and more. Your Mac and other devices must be connected to the same Wi-Fi network.

A Mac computer and AirPlay-capable devices, such as a smart TV, Apple TV, or HomePod small speakers.

Put On Your Preferred Headphones
Put on your preferred headphones and tune in.

To get that full orchestral sound, connect your Mac to a pair of HomePods (or more) or any other AirPlay 2-enabled speakers. Launch Apple Music on your Mac, arrange your playlist, and then choose a speaker from the list by clicking the AirPlay symbol in the player's controls.

The Music app's playback controls. Just next to the volume control is an AirPlay symbol.

If you want to learn more about the world as you eat, try listening to a travel podcast.

Display media on a large screen and enjoy them.

Playing media on a large-screen TV, such as movies or TV programs, is simple. Start the program in the Apple TV app on Mac, then pick your Apple TV or smart TV by clicking the AirPlay video icon in the playing controls.

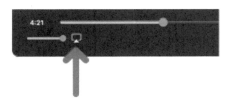

The playback controls in the Apple TV app. Just below the current progress indicator is the AirPlay video icon.

Share your videos

Do you have a fantastic video you found on the internet and want to share it with your friends? You can activate AirPlay in Safari itself.

Using AirPlay mirroring and an Apple TV, you can broadcast what's playing on your Mac, such as a slideshow of wedding images in the images app, on the large screen TV so that everyone can enjoy it. To mirror your Mac's screen to an Apple TV or smart TV, open Control Center from the Mac's menu bar.

Control Center provides access to screen-mirroring solutions like Apple TV.

Your Mac may act as a media player for audio and video from other AirPlay-compatible Apple devices.

Control Your Mac And iPad

Control your Mac and iPad using the same set of keys and mouse.

Using Universal Control, you may share a single set of input devices (keyboard, mouse, trackpad) across up to three different computers, tablets, or smartphones. Things may be dragged from one device to another.

Make sure of the following before using Universal Control:

- You're using a Mac or iPad that we officially support.
- Your iPad runs iOS 15.0 or later, while your Mac runs macOS 12.3.
- All of your devices use the same Apple ID and are protected by two-factor authentication.
- Wi-Fi, Bluetooth®, and Handoff are all enabled in your computer's System Preferences and the iPad's Settings, respectively.

Pair Your Mac With A Nearby Device

Using Universal Control, you may pair your Mac with a nearby device and operate both with a single set of input devices (keyboard, mouse, trackpad).

You may have to re-establish the connection with Universal Control if you don't use it for a while.

Pick one of the options below:

- Move the cursor to the far right or far left of the Mac screen using the mouse or trackpad. If a border pops up on your Mac's screen, just drag your cursor beyond it to continue navigating.
- Select System Preferences from the Apple menu, and then click Displays in the left pane. (It may be necessary to scroll below.) Select a device to link your keyboard and mouse to by clicking the corresponding button under "Add Display" on the right. You can get the cursor to appear on the other device by dragging it beyond the Mac's screen's edge using a mouse or trackpad.
- In the menu bar of your Mac, choose System Preferences, then click Display, and finally, select a device under "Link keyboard and mouse too." You can get the cursor to appear on the other device by dragging it beyond the Mac's screen's edge using a mouse or trackpad.

Which side of the screen you connect your devices to depends on the direction in which you move the pointer while doing so. You may alter this behavior by adjusting the placement of the devices in Displays settings. You may reposition the screen by clicking and dragging its picture.

A Mac may be configured to automatically establish a connection with another Mac or iPad in range.

Select Displays from the sidebar after selecting Apple menu > System Settings. (It may be necessary to scroll below.) When you're ready, go to the right and choose "Automatically reconnect to any nearby Mac or iPad."

Separate Your Mac From All Other Gadgets

Universal Control connections are persistent until one of the connected devices goes to sleep or you manually break them.

1. Select System Preferences from the Apple menu, and then click Displays in the left pane. (It may be necessary to scroll below.)
2. Disconnect by clicking the button to the right of your screen.

Disable The Global Lockdown System

You may prohibit your Mac from communicating with external keyboards and mice by switching off Universal Control.

1. Select System Preferences from the Apple menu, and then click Displays in the left pane. (It may be necessary to scroll below.)
2. Disconnect from all sources of Universal Control: Remove the checkmark from "Allow your pointer and keyboard to move between any nearby Mac or iPad."

- Prevent a link from forming when the mouse is moved near the screen's border: Uncheck the box labeled "Push through the edge of a display to connect to a nearby Mac or iPad."
- To make it simpler to zoom in along the border of the screen, you may configure your Mac to temporarily deactivate Universal Control whenever you zoom in.

Using Apple's Handoff

Using Apple's Handoff, you may continue where you left off.

Whether you're using a Mac, iPhone, iPad, or Apple Watch, Handoff makes it easy to begin working on one device and continue right where you left off on another. If you're replying to an email and you start it on your iPhone, you can complete it in Mail on your Mac. Handoff works with a wide variety of Apple programs, including Calendar, Contacts, Pages, and Safari. Some third-party applications may also function with Handoff.

The Dock symbol for an iPhone app that supports Handoff.

Handoff requires Apple devices to be compatible with the Continuity platform. Your Mac and iOS/iPadOS devices need to have Wi-Fi, Bluetooth®, and Handoff enabled in System Preferences and Settings, respectively. All of your Apple devices must have the same Apple ID.

While Handoff is on, you may utilize Universal Clipboard to easily copy and paste data across devices. Files may be copied from one Mac to another.

Flip the switch for Handoff
In the absence of a dedicated Handoff setting, your device will not be compatible with the service.

- In Mac OS: Click the Apple menu > System Settings > General > AirDrop & Handoff > and toggle the "Allow Handoff between this Mac and your iCloud devices" switch. (It may be necessary to scroll below.)
- If you have an iPad, iPhone, or iPod touch: To enable or disable Handoff, go to Settings > General > AirPlay & Handoff.

- To toggle Enable Handoff on or off on Apple Watch, launch the Apple Watch app on your iPhone and go to My Watch > General.

Changeover in technology

- While using your Mac, the Handoff icon of the app you have open will display on your iPhone (at the bottom of the app switcher) or iPad/iPod touch (at the end of the Dock). Select to continue using the app.
- Connecting an Apple Watch, iPhone, iPad, or Mac: Near the right end of the Dock (or the bottom, depending on the Dock position), the Handoff icon of the program you're using on your iPhone, iPad, iPod touch, or Apple Watch will display on your Mac. Click the icon to continue working in the app.

  Pressing Command-Tab will also take you to the program that displays the Handoff icon.

Use Watch Approval System For Your Mac

Use Apple Watch as a password and approval system for your Mac.

You may use your Apple Watch to unlock your Mac or authorize app requests without entering a password when you have both devices on you at the same time and are close to each other.

Make sure your Mac (released in the middle of 2013 or later) and Apple Watch are both signed in with the same Apple ID and that two-factor authentication is set on for your Apple ID if you want to utilize these capabilities.

Apple Watch may be used for automatic unlocking and approval.

1. Select Touch ID & Password from the sidebar after selecting Apple menu > System Settings. (It may be necessary to scroll below.)
2. Select Apple Watch on the right, and then activate the switch next to your watch's name.

   If you don't have watchOS 6 on your Apple Watch, you can't use this feature.

Macintosh, unlock!
Any key on the keyboard, or the opening of the display on a portable Mac, will bring the computer out of sleep mode. Your Mac is being unlocked, and the process is shown on screen.

Take in app submissions
The Apple Watch will notify you on the Mac that it needs your permission to do anything (such as access passwords, unlock notes or settings, or install apps).

Double-click the side button to approve requests from your Mac.

An Apple Watch displaying a request for authorization from a MacBook Pro.

To accept the job, double-click the Apple Watch's side button.

Select Apple menu > About This Mac, click More Info, and then click System Report at the bottom of the page to see whether your Mac is compatible with Auto Unlock and Approve with Apple Watch. Navigate to the Network subheading in the sidebar, pick Wi-Fi, and check the right-hand column for "Auto Unlock: Supported."

Auto Unlock and Approve with Apple Watch may be enabled for another user on your Mac if their Apple ID supports two-factor authentication and they have the latest version of watchOS loaded on their Apple Watch.

Use Facetime On Your Mac

Use Apple's FaceTime on your Mac to make and take calls.

You may use your Mac instead of your iPhone whenever you need to make or take a call. You can utilize Real-Time Text (RTT) for your phone calls if your carrier offers it, and a notice will pop up on your Mac when someone contacts you.

The New FaceTime window with a person's name in the To box. The bottom alert pane suggests either sending an SMS message or making a phone call using the iPhone.

226

Calls made or received on a Mac will count within your allotted cellular minutes, so keep that in mind.

Make Calls From Your Mac's Applications

1. Sign in to the FaceTime app on your Mac, and check sure the feature is on.
2. If you haven't previously done so, configure your iPhone and Mac to make and receive phone calls.
3. One of the following should be done to make a phone call using a macOS app:

   • To initiate a FaceTime call, choose the option from the drop-down menu after clicking New FaceTime entering the recipient's number in the resulting window, and pressing Return.

   If you already have the person's contact information saved in the Contacts app, you may simply input their name or choose them from the Suggested list.

   You have the option of making an RTT call if you have it set up.

   You may also send an SMS message to invite someone to a call.

   • To dial a contact's number, click the phone icon after selecting that person from your address book.

- You have the option of making an RTT call if you have it set up.
- In Safari, you may dial a number by selecting it and clicking the Call button.
- Email: While hovering over a phone number, choose the desired calling method from the resulting menu.
- To contact a specific location shown on a map, just click its pin.
- To use Spotlight, type the name of an individual or location into the search bar and then choose a result from the suggested searches. Move the cursor over a phone number, then click the Phone button.
- To make a call from your calendar, open an event's details and search for a blue phone number with an arrow next to it. Alternatively, you may click Join to add a FaceTime video call to an existing calendar event.
- To make a call from the reminders list, open the list, click the blue number that is highlighted, and then click Call.
- Retrieve My Launch the People directory and choose a name at random. Just hit "Info," "Contact," and "Call" to get started.

If you can only make phone calls to select persons, the hourglass symbol will display next to their names.

Use Your Mac To Take Calls

When a notice shows in the upper-right corner of your Mac's screen, choose an action from the list provided:

- To answer an incoming call, choose the Accept button.

  If the caller has RTT set up and you'd want to respond in kind, you may do so by selecting RTT when the phone rings.

- You may tell a caller to hold on by clicking the "Decline" button.

  If the call was from an unwanted number, just block the number.

- Use iMessage to politely decline a call: Select Decline from the drop-down menu that appears, then click the arrow next to it and select Reply with Message. You and the person calling you must both be using iMessage at the time.
- Reject a call and schedule a return call: Select a reminder interval of your choosing by clicking the arrow to the right of Decline. A reminder will

be sent to you at the appointed time; upon opening it, you may begin your call by clicking the link provided there.

Accepting or rejecting a call, sending a message, or setting a reminder may all be done via the Touch Bar on a Mac.

Calls from people whose access to your device is limited by Screen Time will show up as missed calls in the FaceTime app or Notification Center.

Control Facetime Call On Your Mac

You can do things like transfer calls to your iPhone or use call waiting while making or receiving calls via FaceTime.

Calls made or received on a Mac will count within your allotted cellular minutes, so keep that in mind.

- To transition to a video call using FaceTime, choose Video from the alert menu (or use the Touch Bar).
- Make an RTT call instead: To respond to the alert, choose RTT.

  If you accidentally leave your microphone on after making a phone call and then switching to an RTT call, you may silence it by clicking the Mute button or by using the Touch Bar.

- If you're already on the phone and another call comes in, you may use call waiting by selecting Hold & Accept from the corresponding menu. To seamlessly transition between calls, use the Switch calls button.

- Connect a new caller to a current one: To merge calls, press Hold & Accept, and then wait for the incoming call to connect.

- If your Mac is within range, you may transfer the call to your iPhone by swiping your finger up from the bottom of the screen to the center and holding it there. Select the Phone icon (located in the screen's footer).

- If you have Wi-Fi Calling enabled on your iPhone, a green bar with the words "Touch to return to call" may show at the top of the screen whenever you unlock it.

- Manage the sound settings by adjusting them.

Control Your Apple ID Preferences

Apple ID preferences may be managed on a Mac.

Your Apple ID allows you access to all Apple services, including the App Store, Apple Music, iCloud, iMessage, FaceTime, and more. After logging in with your Apple ID, you can access your account details, account preferences, payment and shipping details, and more under Apple ID settings.

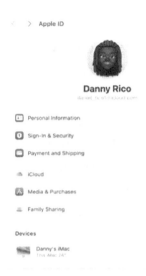

Apple ID preferences, including the user's profile photo and name at the top and their account type choices below.

1. Select System Preferences from the Apple menu, and then look for the section labeled "[your name]" toward the top of the sidebar.

   If your name doesn't appear, choose "Sign in with your Apple ID," input your Apple ID (or a Reachable At email address or phone number that you provided in Apple ID settings), and then enter your password. You can sign up for an Apple ID if you don't already have one.

2. To modify your Mac's Apple ID preferences, choose an item from the list to the right.

- The picture, name, and birthdate linked with your Apple ID may be modified here.
- Here you may modify your Apple ID's sign-in details, such as your email address, password, trusted phone numbers, and security questions and answers.
- You may check the Apple ID's associated payment method and shipment address and make any necessary changes using the respective menus.
- You can configure iCloud+ features, manage your iCloud storage, and decide which iCloud functions you wish to utilize using these choices.
- You may modify your account information, and subscriptions, and download and buy prerequisites here.
- With Family Sharing, up to five members of your immediate family may access and share your subscriptions, purchases, location, and more.
- Devices: This is where you can see and control the devices authorized to use your Apple ID.
- When you're done using your Apple ID, sign out.
- Review the Apple Privacy Policy that is in place to safeguard your Apple ID information.

Put Your Mac's Files In iCloud Drive

You may upload any kind of file to iCloud Drive, and then access it from any of your devices or the online interface at iCloud.com.

iCloud Drive is compatible with Macs running OS X 10.10 or later, iOS 8 or later, iPadOS, and Windows PCs running iCloud for Windows (Windows 7 or later needed). Devices must meet minimum system requirements and use the same Apple ID for sign-in.

Documents and data on devices that do not have iCloud Drive enabled will not be synced with those on devices that do have iCloud Drive enabled.

Create A Drive In iCloud

If you haven't yet set up iCloud Drive on this Mac, you can do so immediately via iCloud settings.

1. Select System Preferences from the Apple menu, then look for the sidebar with your name at the top.

   Click "Sign in with your Apple ID," input your Apple ID (or a Reachable At email address or phone number that you entered in Apple ID settings), and your password if your name doesn't appear. You can sign up for an Apple ID if you don't already have one.

2. To enable iCloud Drive syncing on your Mac, go to the iCloud menu on the right and click it.
3. Simply select the final button.

Put your files on iCloud Drive, including Desktop and Documents.

You may set it up such that iCloud Drive automatically backs up anything in your "Desktop" and "Documents" folders. That way, you may store files precisely where you regularly save them, and they become accessible on all your devices including iCloud.com.

1. Select System Preferences from the Apple menu, then look for the sidebar labeled "[your name]" and select it.

   Click "Sign in with your Apple ID," input your Apple ID (or a Reachable At email address or phone number that you entered in Apple ID settings), and your password if your name doesn't appear. You can sign up for an Apple ID if you don't already have one.

2. To activate iCloud Drive, go to the right pane and activate iCloud before proceeding.

3. Allow the Desktop and Documents to appear.
4. Simply select the final button.

After you switch on Desktop & Documents Folders, your Desktop and Documents folders are migrated into iCloud Drive. They also display in the iCloud part of the Finder sidebar on your Mac, and the Files app on your iPhone or iPad.

Quickly check the iCloud Drive syncing progress on your Mac. Move the cursor over iCloud Drive in the Finder sidebar, then click the status or information icon.

If you can't transfer or save a document to iCloud Drive

If you can't transfer or save a document to iCloud Drive, your iCloud storage capacity may be filled. The document remains on your Mac and is uploaded to iCloud Drive as space becomes available.

iCloud Drive collaborates with other iCloud services, like as iCloud Photos and iCloud Backup for iOS and iPadOS devices, as well as iCloud Mail and its attachments.

To acquire additional room, do the following:

- Upgrade your storage. See Manage iCloud storage.
- Remove stuff you don't need to save in iCloud Drive.

Collaborate On Data With Others

You may use iCloud to store, sync, and collaborate on data with others.

Sharing files and folders with others in iCloud Drive makes it easy to work on projects as a group. The individuals you invite may download the shared objects from iCloud to any of their devices, where they can see them and—depending on the rights you set—collaborate. You may notice any changes the next time you access the files on your Mac.

iCloud Drive folder sharing is only available on devices running macOS 10.15.4 or later, iOS 13.4 or later, or iCloud for Windows 11.1.

Reminders, Safari, Keynote, Pages, and Numbers are just a few of the applications that use iCloud's cloud storage and collaboration features.

Share documents with others and encourage feedback and edits.

1. On a Mac, you may perform one of the following to invite others to work together on a set of files or a set of folders:

   - To share a file or folder, open a Finder window by clicking its icon on the Dock, go to iCloud Drive in the left pane, pick the item you want to share, and finally, click the Share button.

   - To share anything on your desktop, right-click it while holding down the Control key, and then choose **Share**.

   A file or folder must be stored in iCloud Drive if you want to work on it with others.

2. From the drop-down option, choose Collaborate.

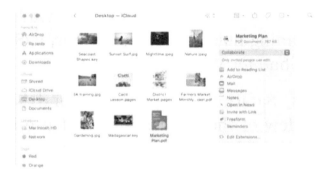

A Finder window holding files and folders. From the option that appears when you click Share, choose Collaborate.

3. To restrict changes to certain individuals, choose "Only invited people can edit." under Collaborate. Then, select the appropriate option from the drop-down menu that appears under "Who can access":

  - To a select few: Confine access to the folder or file to invited users only.
  - Whoever has the URL: Don't restrict access to the file or folder based on who received the link. If you choose this, those you invite will be able to share the link with others and provide access to others who weren't originally invited.

4. Select one of the following options from the pull-down menu that appears when you click Permissions:

  - Allows for Variation: Allow others you invite to read and alter the contents of the file or folder.
  - Access is limited to viewing only; invited users can't make any changes to the file or folder.

5. To make it possible for anybody with access to the file or folder to ask others to join in on the sharing, click the "Allow others to invite" button. Uncheck the option if you don't want other people to have access to the folder or file.

6. Use either Mail or Messages to send the invitation, or make a link to the shared file and send it.

If you share a file or folder on iCloud with others and they accept your invitation, they will be able to access it from any device. If you give someone permission to edit a file on your Mac, the changes will be visible the next time you access the file.

Only the individuals you specifically invite may see the contents of a shared folder. Changing the permissions on a single file inside a shared folder is not possible, only the folder's overall permissions.

If you want to share a file or folder with someone but don't want to work together on it, you may do so by Control-clicking the item in the Finder or on the desktop, selecting Share from the drop-down menu, and then selecting Send Copy from the pop-up menu.

Join a group that has been given access to a shared folder

- To see the shared item in the Finder and have it uploaded to iCloud Drive on your Mac, click the link you got and then click Open.

If you've been invited to access a shared file or folder, you may find it in the following locations:

- When using iCloud Drive on a Mac
- Your iPhone, iPad, or iPod touch with iOS 11 or later with the Files app installed.
- The iCloud website
- To use iCloud on a Windows PC

If you have editing permissions, you may access the shared object in any app that supports it and make changes. The next time someone who has access to the item accesses it, they will see the most recent updates.

Modify the permissions on a shared file or folder at any time.

You can't modify the sharing settings for a specific file inside a shared folder. The folder's parameters must be modified.

1. Open a Finder window by clicking the Finder icon in the Dock, and then go to iCloud Drive by clicking the iCloud Drive button in the window's sidebar.
2. Right-click the folder or file with the Control key, and choose Manage Shared File or Manage Shared Folder, respectively.

3. To send a link to several recipients, choose Add as your action.
    - To send the shared item to a friend, copy the link and paste it into an email. Select the link and press the copy button. Just copy the URL and paste it into your chat, email, or other program.
    - Modify the download permissions: Select "Only people you invite" from the drop-down menu to restrict access to those you specifically invite, or "Anyone with the link" to make it available to anybody who has the link.
    - Set whether or not others may make changes to the shared document: To provide people editing privileges, choose "can make changes" from the pull-down option just underneath Permissions; alternatively, select "can view only" to grant only read privileges.
    - Selecting "Anyone can add more people" changes the permissions so that anybody with access to the item may invite others. If you don't check this box, nobody but you will be able to send invitations.
    - Modify someone's individual sharing preferences: Place the mouse cursor where you'd want to make changes, and then click.

- Don't send a file to that person anymore: Place the mouse cursor over their name, click, and choose Revoke Access.

Simply choose the last button.
Take care of your shared files in one place.

The Shared folder in the Finder sidebar makes it easy to see what you and others have shared. Follow these steps to organize the shared folders in your account:

1. Launch Finder from the Dock, then choose Shared from the window's sidebar to access shared folders and files on your Mac.
2. Select Shared By from the toolbar's pop-up Grouping option.

You can see the Grouping pop-up menu open and the Shared By option chosen since the Grouping

symbol is highlighted in the Finder window's toolbar.

This window lists all of the shared folders and files, organized into groups according to who shared them.

This is a Finder window with the Shared folder selected in the sidebar, and the shared objects are shown on the right.

Delete A Shared Folder Or File

1. Open a Finder window by clicking the Finder icon in the Dock, and then go to iCloud Drive by clicking the iCloud Drive button in the window's sidebar.
2. Use the Control>Shared File or Shared Folder> menus to administer the shared object.
3. You may stop sharing by clicking the Stop Sharing button.

- Don't tell that individual anymore: To revoke a user's access, roll the mouse over their name, click, and choose the corresponding option.
- To prevent others from accessing a file or folder, you may either remove it from iCloud Drive or delete it.

You can no longer view the shared files by the participants once you have stopped sharing or deleted the shared folder.

If the person you're sharing with also creates a duplicate, they'll be able to keep using it even after you've stopped sharing.

Made in United States
Troutdale, OR
11/18/2023

14718100R00146